SURVIVING CORRUPTION

BY DICK RICHARDS

Friesenpress

Suite 300 - 990 Fort St
Victoria, BC, V8V 3K2
Canada

www.friesenpress.com

Copyright © 2020 by Dick Richards
First Edition — 2020

All rights reserved.

No part of this publication may be reproduced in any form, or by any means, electronic or mechanical, including photocopying, recording, or any information browsing, storage, or retrieval system, without permission in writing from FriesenPress.

ISBN
978-1-5255-7903-5 (Hardcover)
978-1-5255-7904-2 (Paperback)
978-1-5255-7905-9 (Ebook)

Biography & Autobiography, Law Enforcement

Distributed to the trade by The Ingram Book Company

Table of Contents

Introduction v

Part One:
My Younger Years 1

Part Two:
Boarding School 19

Part Three:
Teenage Punk 25

Part Four:
Out on My Own 55

Part Five:
Life After Marriage 69

Part Six:
Now I'm a Cop 93

Part Seven:
Joined The Fire Department 161

Part Eight:
Illness, Entrepreneurial Work, and Fun 197

Part Nine:
Border Services Officer on the 'Coast' 225

Part Ten:
Final Years at the Border 'Inland' 265

Part Eleven:
Life After Retirement 285

Last Part:
That's All Folks 289

Introduction

THIS IS A book of short stories – all of which are true. It is about my life which has always involved some form of rebellion or corruption. Sometimes I was on the right side of the law, and sometimes I wasn't. Either way, I always had the ability to fly under the radar of the legal system and most employers, including law enforcement. I probably should have spent some time in jail, but I've never been caught at anything other than speeding and fighting. I think I have been lucky or I have a diabolical mind. You decide: luck or creativity?

I have been present when people have died, and it takes it a toll. I have been at axe and shooting murder scenes; a baby's death by fire; a head run over by a truck; several suicide victims by hanging, shotgun, and one who later jumped to her death; heart attacks and car accidents. A few of the stories aren't pleasant, so you've been warned.

I have chosen to withhold employer identification and I use fake names in my stories. I have written this book under the pseudonym Dick Richards.

I was raised in a big city in the northwest and came from a dysfunctional middle class family. I have three siblings, none of whom I have anything to do with because when my parents divorced, they were close to my mother and I was close to my dad.

For the most part, my dad and I were 'best friends'. My mother looked out for herself over everyone else. Family was not important to her. Money was! My mom and I were never very close. My wife and I were both eighteen years old when we met. We're in our seventies now and still deeply in love. My stories span over 65 years. After marriage I changed jobs many times. I have been a truck driver; police officer; big city fire department; small fire department; border officer; drug dog handler; intelligence officer; entrepreneur and more.

Most of my jobs were 4 days on and 4 days off so I had multiple part time jobs to fill my time off. My part time gigs were locksmith, private investigator, repo agent, ambulance attendant, corrections officer, truck driver and armored car driver. I had several self employed part-time occupations as well. My wife and I also flipped houses.

Part One:
My Younger Years

WHAT KIND OF kid gets involved in corruption and aggressive/rebellious behavior almost his entire life? In my case, I'll chalk it up to an abusive mother. When my mother died she left a diary behind, and I had the opportunity to browse through it. It was mostly written on loose pages that were in several boxes, so it wasn't possible to read everything, but I managed to read a number of pages where she wrote that she resented me. I guess I'm a bit warped because it actually flattered me.

My parents met in WW2 and married over sea. My mother was an unusual person, not easily approachable and very opinionated.

My sister was a year older than me and we were close as pre schoolers, but I have few memories of her. My two brothers were 5 and 6 years younger than me and after they were born, every family picture I saw had no smiles on any faces. I don't know why (financial reasons, infidelity, incompatible). I have no idea!

She also wrote in her diary that when I was born, my dad spent too much time with me and she hated it. As a young child, I played in the yard with the kid next door. God forbid! She complained to my dad about me and my friend playing on the lawn all the time, and she wanted him to discipline me for it. He wouldn't, so she wrote to my uncle who was a priest in an effort to gain support from him to see things her way. Struck out again! Her dislike for me was gaining momentum and her demeanor deteriorated more every year.

I believe I was born aggressive and that might have had something to do with our personality clashes.

I was born in a small town where my dad and his brother owned the only grocery store. Eventually, our family moved to a big city further west. Dad got a job there driving a horse drawn milk wagon.

My parents bought a house under a veteran plan and by the time I was about four years old, I was pretty independent. My sister and I frequently played outside within a short distance from our house. One day, I noticed the biggest dog I'd ever seen, and it was running toward us. My first thought was that we were going to get eaten. So I yelled at my sister to run, then I bolted for home with her right behind me.

I glanced back and saw the dog was still coming after us. A wooden stick was lying on the side of the road, so I picked it up and after my sister ran by, I was ready for battle with a weapon in hand. The dog approached me, and I whacked it on the head as hard as I could.

The poor dog ran off yelping and I ran home, pumped with adrenaline, scared and shaking. It was probably a friendly dog looking to play, but my imagination got carried away. To me, any dog bigger than a cat looked huge.

I didn't always have the upper hand over animals though. Sometimes they came out on top. When I was about ten years old, my dad took me to the zoo where some small monkeys were contained behind glass. I began to tease one of those monkeys. The monkey turned his back to me. Then he turned his head around to look at me, and I know he was looking right at me! He lifted his tail and pointed to his ass with his index finger. I might not have been wise to the ways of the world, but I did know when I was being insulted. People nearby burst out laughing, and I took off out of there blushing. That damn monkey had just called me an asshole. To this day, I cannot understand how a monkey knew how to totally embarrass a kid, and believe me, I was embarrassed. It was an unforgettable moment in my life.

My parents were close to my uncle and aunt. I was eleven, and two of their boys were my age. We would go out and look for our own entertainment when our parents visited to play cards. One afternoon when they were over, we thought it would be a good idea to go and pick crab apples from the neighbor's tree. Then we'd hide in the bushes across a nearby street and throw them at passing cars.

That was a lot of fun until one of the cars we hit came to a screeching halt, and the driver jumped out and ran toward the bushes where we were hiding. I was way back in the bushes with my younger cousin, but my older cousin was slightly visible and the guy spotted him. He grabbed him, pulled him out, and started yelling at him and roughed him up a little. One of the neighbors nearby heard the commotion and he came over and shouted at the guy to let the kid go.

Luckily, neither of them saw the two of us hiding quietly, so we remained still and scared. The guy in the car left soon afterward. The neighbor went home and my cousins, and I went back to my house quite relieved. That pretty much put a stop to our crab apple throwing, but we learned a lesson from it.

Unfortunately, it wasn't enough of a lesson to prevent us from stealing tomatoes. My younger cousin and I walked by a house that had a few tomato plants growing beside the steps near the front door. They were easy to spot, being bright red and a fair size. We each picked a couple of tomatoes, and in a "brain fart" moment, threw them at the door of his house.

The homeowner heard the tomatoes hit the door and came out to investigate. His tomatoes were crushed on his doorstep, and when he saw us running away, he gave chase. Holy crap! We ran and ran, but the guy wouldn't quit. He kept coming. Then we spotted a thistle field. The thistles were almost waist high and covered an acre of land.

We ran through the field, and damn, did those thistles ever hurt! It felt like our legs were on fire. Still, the guy kept on coming. We couldn't believe it, but finally, halfway through the field, he gave up and retreated. Both my cousin and I were so glad to finally get some relief from the pain. We were now able to walk slowly to the other side. Another lesson learned. With all this learning, we could actually be quite smart some day.

However there was still much more to learn! In the winter, after our Cub (a junior edition of the Boy Scouts) meeting, we'd hang around in a group on our way home with each kid breaking off as we passed their house. Icy roads and snow were abundant. We learned that if we saw a car coming, and one of us pretended he needed to cross the street, the car would stop for him. While the driver watched the kid cross, the rest of us would run up behind the car and crouch down behind the vehicle where the driver couldn't see us.

Then, when he took off, we were holding on to the car's bumper, and we literally skied behind the car in our shoes or boots. Of course, the roads had to be slippery enough to indulge in this brilliant sport! Sometimes we went more then a block at over 30 mph before letting go. "Bumper skiing" we called it. Sometimes the driver would see us and stop the car. Then we'd run off, but they rarely got out of their cars.

In a different stunt, I climbed onto a high roof at the local community hall. It was quite sloped, but at the time, there was a shed close to it that allowed easy access to the building's roof. I made it all the way to the top when some do-gooder saw me and called me down. I refused to come down, but when he said he was going to call the police I did so reluctantly.

I instantly started planning my escape. The guy was probably a good guy concerned about my safety and all, but jeez, he was taking this matter a little too seriously. He asked me where I lived because he was going to speak with my parents. I pointed to a house across the street but down three houses from the corner. He told me to go home, and he'd drive over in his car.

I ran to that house, which actually wasn't mine because I lived a block further down the alley. When I went into the yard, I quickly went through the front gate and latched it behind me. Then I walked down the side of the house while he was getting out of his car.

As soon as I was out of his sight I ran like hell out the back gate and down the alley behind all the high bushes. I ran into my own back yard and never saw him after that. He must have felt awfully stupid when he knocked on the door of that place and complained about their boy climbing on a high roof. They would have thought he was nuts. I was scared but still laughing thinking about it all.

I was also a handful at home. My mom had two locked steamer trunks in the basement. She claimed sole ownership over them and even my dad didn't have a key. I often wondered what was in those trunks, so one day I spent a bit of time picking the locks.

"Wow!" There were mostly items made of fabric, but there were also a few boxes of Belgium licorice and some marzipan candy in there. I enjoyed taking a few of the licorice whenever I got the urge, but the marzipan was horrible. The best part of the cache was a box full of Canadian silver dollars Mom was apparently collecting. I helped myself to several of those as well. I'm not sure if she ever noticed because I was never challenged. But perhaps she couldn't challenge me on it because Dad might not have known about them. Since there was quite a large quantity of them, she probably didn't miss the ones I took.

Another time, I was playing with my BB gun in the back yard and using the hydro meter as a target. I didn't realize the glass over the meter was so thin. As a result, the BB's left bull's-eye-type glass dings each time I hit it, and after several hits, splinters of glass jammed the meter mechanism. The meter then stopped recording hydro use.

To make up for the loss, Hydro charged us the same amount as the harshest winter month of the previous year. In my defense, I really had no idea the glass was breaking because all the BB's appeared to be bouncing off, and I wasn't close enough to see the dings. My mother was livid.

We also used to take our BB rifles to boy-scout camp sessions, and I remember three of us standing on either side of a bridge armed with those rifles and shooting at each other. The BB's stung when they hit, and it wasn't very long before one of the boys fired a BB that stuck in the eyebrow of another boy on the other side. We then realized that it could've hit an eye, so we stopped doing it and just shot at birds.

I'm not sure where or when I picked up all or any of my undesirable practices. It might have been a psychological flaw, but I think it was to survive, and surviving with money was what I preferred. Going back almost as far as I can remember, I've always found ways to make a few dollars.

My mother was extremely frugal. Just to give you an example of how frugal she was, we kids got 25 cents a week allowance, two dollars during parade week (to ride on rides at the carnival), and five dollars for birthdays. There was a "no Santa Claus" clause in our house. However, for Christmas we could pick any item out of a catalogue valued at under ten dollars. Then when it arrived, we had to wrap our own present and put it under the tree. We also didn't celebrate Easter and Thanksgiving, and there were no birthday cakes either.

When I was twelve years old, I found that I could make more money than a newspaper delivery boy who earned only one or two pennies per newspaper and work less for it. I sold weekly magazines for 75 cents and my share was 25 cents a copy. That way I delivered to less than 10% of the customer base that a newspaper delivery boy did and my commission and tips were much higher.

Then I discovered I could make even more money by carrying golf clubs as a caddy for rich guys at an elite golf course, so I quit my job with the weekly magazine and "accidentally" forgot to submit their 50 cent portion of the 75 cents collected per magazine. I guess for them, following up was more trouble than they felt it was worth, so I was able to keep the money for that final week. I even received a "gift" from them. It was a Swiss army knife in a holster.

That knife turned out to be bad karma though. I put the holster on the front of my belt and had the knife blade open and protruding downward through the opening at the bottom. That was stupid because when I jumped over a log, the knife blade plunged into my thigh. After that I got to say I had been stabbed, but that might have been a bit misleading.

As a new caddy, I found that the caddy shack was normally filled with young lads eager to caddy. The ages of the boys ranged from twelve years old to about seventeen or eighteen. I watched the temperaments of the different boys who, in that atmosphere, tended to bully one another. I knew that the older and bigger boys were no match and should be left alone even if they provoked you to try and get you to react. There were many fights in that caddy shack and anyone caught fighting was sent home and was no longer permitted to caddy.

After I caddied for a few weeks, I learned to estimate the distances from my client's ball to the green, and I'd pull the correct club out of the bag before my client asked for it. When you do that, it often generated a higher tip at the end of the game, especially if your client won low score. Sometimes the tips were as high as $10 for a game, and some days, I would do two rounds a day especially on weekends. That was a big money for a twelve year old.

I belonged to the Boy Scouts at that time, and in the winter, there was no golf income. Over the Christmas season, I volunteered to sell Christmas trees at our Boy Scout lot. It was quite easy to sell a tree and pocket 100% of the proceeds when the scoutmasters were in the trailer and not paying attention. I made myself a pretty nice wage for a couple of seasons until I got kicked out of Boy Scouts after a summer camp, for raiding a tent the scoutmasters used and stealing some cigarettes.

One year I picked out a watch from the Christmas catalogue, and even at that time, a nine-dollar-watch was not a quality piece, so I used my Christmas tree money to buy a nice watch at the drugstore for thirty dollars. I exchanged it with the one I had wrapped and put the present back under the tree. When I opened it at Christmas, no one was any wiser. Furthermore, no one in the family even bothered to ask to see my new watch because Christmas spirit in our house was non-existent and nobody really gave a shit. I threw the other watch up into the ceiling above my downstairs bedroom, and I wouldn't be surprised if it was still there to this day.

In elementary school I ended up actually passing to grade eight from grade seven with failing grades. My average grade for the year was only 17%, but the elementary school probably had enough of me, so they passed me into grade eight to get rid of me. The fact that my teacher had it in for me also might have contributed. He would have wanted me gone as well.

I did pretty well in school from grades one through six, but every report card indicated I talked too much with the other kids in class. Grade seven, on the other hand, was a game changer. We had an Australian exchange teacher who was an idiot and a pervert. During physical education class, he would make all the kids, both boys and girls, do somersaults over a padded mat. He would kneel down on the mat and "assist" the girls in doing the somersaults. It was evident he was doing this to pleasure himself because before long he had a boner bulging in his pants. In those days there was no education or information about perverts, so not knowing any better, we boys just chuckled behind his back and pointed it out to each other. The kids all hated him.

Once I put a whole box of thumbtacks on his chair and pushed the chair back under his desk so he couldn't see them. As usual, he pulled the chair out while talking to us and looking out at the class so he didn't notice them until he sat down. He didn't say anything, but he got up very quickly and his face turned bright red. I think he might have suspected I had done it because he was pretty hard on me from then on. He probably noticed me snickering.

One time, he saw me take a note from a classmate and told me to bring it to him. I refused, so he strapped me with a conveyor belt strap seven times in a row. I got three hits on each hand, and each time, he'd say to me in his Australian accent, "UP ON THE FLOOR." Then he had me go back to sit at my desk, and he'd ask for the note again. Each time he asked, I refused, then again, "UP ON THE FLOOR."

Even after seven innings, I wasn't going to let the prick win. Doing the math, it equates to 21 hits on each hand to a kid in grade seven, just thirteen years old, simply because someone had passed a note to me and I would not give it to him.

I hung around with a couple of bad boys back then – Ray and Ron, who were the two biggest boys in the class. Apparently I had impressed them with my stubbornness when I refused to comply and hand over my note to the abusive teacher. It was great hanging around with them because everyone in the class feared them. Unfortunately, it turned me into a bit of a bully, and I started to persistently bother one individual in particular by pushing him around here and there. That was to come to a sudden end shortly thereafter.

He could only take so much, and one day when I was poking at him and making fun of him, he blindsided me. He punched me right in the face with his fist. It immediately gave me a tremendous amount of respect for him, and I never bothered him again. Later in life when I had kids and a couple of my boys told me that they were being bullied, I remembered this lesson. I told them to hit the offender in the nose as hard as they could with a closed fist and try to break his nose or at least make him bleed.

"I guarantee he'll never bother you again. You might get a beating following the punch, but it will be worth it because he will leave you alone after that." It worked for me so I assumed it would work for them. Two of my boys had the opportunity to give it a try, and it worked very well for both of them. One of them did suffer backlash after the punch, but years later, the boy who he hit, told him how shocked he was when he got blindsided. He also learned a life lesson from it because he did leave my son alone after that. It really works well!

Whenever the Australian exchange teacher left the classroom all hell would break loose in the class. My two new friends thought it would be quite funny to throw me out the window into the bushes outside the classroom. It was on the ground floor, so it wouldn't hurt me and the class would appreciate the prank. They threw me out the window and then closed and locked it so I couldn't get back in.

I had to sneak past the principal's office and down the hall to get back into class without getting caught. I managed to get back undetected, but I wasn't happy with the stunt and from then on I avoided the two of them. Sometimes you think you have friends, and sometimes you learn you don't.

My mother often beat on me with heavy wooden spoon for things I'd done like eating in the living room or taking too much time in the bathroom – silly little things like that. I admit I was no angel, but after a while, my dislike for her was increasing and she noticed it so the abuse increased.

Dad would often go for a nap. I would raid his wallet while he was sleeping. I took a couple of bucks out of it one day and took one of my little brothers to the dairy place for a milkshake. I made the mistake of telling my brother that I took money out of Dad's wallet and was paying for his milkshake with it. He told Dad and I got tuned up for doing it. Lesson learned.

In grade eight, the school I was attending was only a few blocks from a major grocery store. My friend Norm and I used to go there every lunch hour to steal cigarettes and chocolate bars and then sell them to other classmates. He would go to the candy counter and grab a few bars, and I would cut through an unoccupied teller station where the cigarettes were kept and grab a few packages from behind the display.

That went on for months, but eventually the store staff figured out it was kids from the school who were taking all the cigarettes, so when kids entered the store at lunchtime, they started to keep an eye on them. The store staff watched Norm scoop some chocolate bars, and they thought he also had stolen some cigarettes (which, of course, I had just taken but they didn't see me). They grabbed him when he was leaving the store, but I had already left with my booty and gone to our predetermined meeting place to wait for him.

That should have been my last day of criminal activity because it scared the hell out of me. Norm had to endure the wrath of his parents and the school's administrators. However, I picked up the habit again the following year.

I had a teacher who spoke French and went to the same church as my mom and dad. Mom took a liking to him because they both spoke French, and she invited him over to our house, usually after church on Sundays.

Mom would criticize my sister and me in front of him, severely belittling us. She would point at my sister's hair and say to this teacher, "Just look at how sloppy she is; she can't even comb her hair." Mom was ruthless and flung insults at both of us. It didn't bother me too much, but my sister developed schizophrenia later in life. I don't know if that had anything to do with her getting it though.

My dad, who didn't speak any French, didn't want to visit with Mom and the teacher and sat in the living room. I usually stayed in the room with Dad. If I stayed out of her sight, she couldn't verbally go after me or Dad would defend me.

Mom had a metal filing cabinet upstairs (in addition to the trunks in the basement) in which she kept some of her cherished valuables such as candy, bus tickets, etc. Dad was not privy to a key for that cabinet either. I didn't chance taking any of the stuff in there because she was in it every day and would notice if I took anything. It was just a challenge to get in there being as it was so well guarded.

In those days, kids were using yellow paper bus tickets to ride a transit bus. They were the same size and texture as the rolls of draw tickets often sold at functions to offer a chance to win on a 50/50 draw.

I realized that if you softened those tickets up a bit by bending them one way and then another several times, you could pull them apart. This would net two whole tickets, each with printing on one side and a blank face on the other side. I used these on the bus to go to school. I had to drop them into a glass collection receptacle while the bus driver watched to see if everyone paid as they entered.

It was best to board the bus between several people entering at the same stop, which made it more difficult for the driver to watch what everyone was dropping in the collection box. It was a mixture of coin and yellow and purple (adult) bus tickets. In two weeks I could net one week of tickets that had printing on both sides. That way, I could sell the tickets that hadn't been tampered with to other students for half price. Kids were allowed to use those tickets every day including weekends.

One sharp-eyed bus driver, who probably had been given a heads-up from his accounting section about those modified tickets, caught me when one of my tickets landed at the bottom of the collection box with the blank side up. I was boarding the bus with about fifteen other kids, but he quickly got out of his seat, caught me halfway down the aisle, and confronted me about the ticket. He wrote down the name and address that I gave him in a notebook and was likely going to let transit security follow up on the deception. Good thing I gave him the alias that I used occasionally as well as a phony address that was a vacant lot. Then I avoided taking the bus for a few weeks and used my bicycle.

Things continued to get worse at home and one Saturday, when Dad was working overtime, Mom came after me again and began relentlessly hitting me. I can't remember what I had done because hitting me was a common occurrence. When I tried to defend myself, she went berserk and came at me even harder – sometimes with that wooden spoon and other times with an open hand, a shoe, a closed fist, or a belt.

This time I tried to avoid her by locking myself in the only bathroom in the house. She pounded on the door yelling at me to open it. I refused, so she said she was going to burn the door down. I held my ground and thought to myself, Yah, sure you will! Damned if she didn't go get some matches. She lit them up one after another and held them under the bathroom door.

Holy crap, she is really going to do it, I thought. The bathroom window was about twelve feet above ground level, so I quietly unlocked the door after first opening the window, and then I jumped out. I survived the jump with no problem!

By unlocking the door, I don't mean just releasing the privacy lock. A privacy lock would not have prevented her from entering. She would only need a nail to unlock it. However, there was a storage closet close to the bathroom door with a door knob that lined up perfectly with the knob on the bathroom door. The storage closet was quite narrow, and I discovered if I placed the bathroom scale a certain way, I could bind the two knobs tight together. That prevented anyone from entering by using a nail or even if they tried to kick the door in.

I quietly took the scale out of my creative locking position to unjam the door. If I left the scale there, the only way to get back into the bathroom would have been with a twelve-foot ladder to crawl back in through the window.

After going out the window, I walked about two miles to where Dad worked. I told him Mom was going to burn down the house because she was lighting matches under bathroom door.

I explained how hostile she was. I stayed with him until he finished his work day, and then he drove us both home. I quickly went down to my basement bedroom and locked myself in while they had a yelling spat with one another. That day probably determined that I would be sent off to private school for a year at just thirteen years old.

Part Two:
Boarding School

THAT PRIVATE SCHOOL was a hellhole run by a bunch of Christian monks who seemed to love physically abusing young boys. In hindsight, I realize I was probably a problem child and had some punishment coming, but I suffered many beatings there by the Christian Brothers. I'm sure I was a handful, but I can't really remember what I did to warrant a Brother recruiting five or six boys to hold me and pull down my pants. Then the Brother beat me with the handle of a golf club, delivering ten harsh hits to my naked ass. I should mention I was never sexually abused at the private boarding school, but I was often punched, slapped, or beaten with sticks, a belt, or a golf club handle.

While the Brothers ran the place, I learned how to shoplift without getting caught and when, where, and how to fight as well as how to win a fight. That private school boarded just under fifty kids my age and about fifty older ones on the floor below us.

When I was at that school, my friend Peter and I had quite a shoplifting system. Before entering a store we would separate. One of us would walk between two cash registers that weren't being used and snatch a paper bag. Then as planned, the bag was dropped off "let's say" in canned goods by the corn in aisle three. The other would enter the store with other customers so as not to attract attention, and if the coast was clear, would take four or five packages of cigarettes from behind the cash register. That's where the stores kept them back then.

He'd then take them to the corn in aisle #3 and leave them near the bag. That way if he was challenged, he could say he was going to buy them but realized he forgot his money so he just put them down there. If the store employees saw him take the cigarettes but did not see him put them down, they might stop him at the door but only to be disappointed because he no longer had them. The other kept an eye on the cigarettes for a while, and once he was sure no one from the store was aware they were there, he would put them in the bag and leave the store. It appeared to be a legitimate purchase because it was now in a store bag.

We got so good at stealing jujubes, cigarettes, and even an iron one time that the other boys back in the boarding school put in orders for. What they paid us for those items supplemented our two-dollar weekly allowance.

When we had enough money to buy a case of beer, we would walk all the way to the liquor store downtown, which was a long way from the school. Then we would find a homeless street person. We'd convince him to go in and buy us beer. In exchange for that service we would allow him to buy himself a bottle of wine.

That worked quite well eight times out of ten. The other two times we had to chase the guy down when he was leaving the store with two or three bottles of wine instead of our case of beer. We'd have to physically overpower him to take whatever he bought. For that reason it was always best to pick a small or old homeless person who would be much easier to thump out, if they screwed us over.

That boarding school was where I learned to fight because out of the forty-five or so boys in my dorm about twenty of them were Mexican. Those Mexican boys all stuck together, so if you fought with one, you fought with them all.

One of the Christian Brothers there was probably a pedophile because he would line us all up in the morning to have our showers. We'd be standing there naked waiting our turn while holding our towels. Most covered themselves with the towels, but he was way too interested. The Mexicans were like a gang and occasionally would whip or flick the towels at us. It stung when the towel hit you on the leg or anywhere else on the naked body.

One time, one of the bigger Mexican boys flicked me with his towel, and I lost my temper so I hit him and he got a nosebleed. My action was followed by one of the Brothers hitting me in the face. He drew blood as well and actually broke my nose. Hitting that Mexican kid was a good choice at the time because it generated a lot of respect from the Mexicans. Actually, after that I had no problem with them.

Fighting was one of the more popular activities in that school. I took boxing there too and learned some of the techniques. I quit after five or six sessions though because when I got whacked in the head, even with a boxing glove, I usually got a sinus headache. When I fought on the street, I didn't get hit in the head very much so I enjoyed that a lot more. Street fighting was all about fist and elbow fighting and kicking with pointed-toed shoes. At that time, we all bought pointed shoes with metal covering the tips of the shoes. It was a fad.

The dorm contained twenty-six bunk beds. There were almost fifty of us in a single dorm. There were another fifty senior kids down one floor, on the second floor.

I'm in the front row of the picture, fifth from the left.

The Christian Brothers also made us attend church every morning before breakfast. When they came in clapping to wake us up in the morning, we would have to roll out of bed immediately and kneel on the side of the lower bunk. Then they would lead us in a prayer: "Clap, clap, clap, clap, clap. Our Father, who art in heaven, hallowed be thy name, thy kingdom come…"

If you didn't kneel right away, you got whipped with a leather belt. Then we had a half hour to shower and dress. After that we were marched single file across the street to the Catholic Church to attend morning church service. EVERY FREAKING DAY!

Then we'd march single file back to the college to the cafeteria for breakfast. The food was pretty good, I have to say. You took a plate at the start of the line and stopped at the station with the food you liked best. The kitchen staff either plopped a serving on your plate or you took a pastry, pancakes, or whatever you wanted from the buffet line.

Often times, after class we would sneak into the church, hide in the upper balcony, and wait for old people to come in. They would kneel in front of a rack of candles and drop money into the money slot and then light a candle and say a prayer. After they left, we'd go right to the money box. It had five sides, and the sixth side on the right end of the box was open so you simply reached in and scooped out the coins. It supplemented our allowance.

On the weekends I mostly stayed in the college (only a few of us remained on weekends). We went into the locker area by the school classrooms and picked locks on lockers occupied by day students who lived in the surrounding neighborhoods. It was easy booty. I even netted a nice school jacket that I thought was pretty cool. I wore it a lot because there was no way the previous owner could possibly check all the jackets being worn by students.

We also raided the cafeteria cooler because no one was in there working on the weekends. I know… it's all very bad behavior. I was probably destined for a jail cell. After meeting my wife, she tried to straighten me out and was successful in many ways, but I've never been one to avoid all temptation.

At the boarding school we'd often sneak out at night and climb fences to access swimming pools of nearby neighbors. Three of us were in one of the pools swimming when all of a sudden the lights all came on everywhere! The speed at which we got out of the pool, grabbed our clothing, threw it over the fence, and then went over ourselves was nothing short of amazing. We just couldn't be caught because it would have been a beating with a golf club handle or even a fist in the face from one of the Brothers.

Part Three:
Teenage Punk

WHEN I RETURNED home after a year at boarding school, my parents split up. My return home probably had a lot to do with them separating. Dad felt so bad about sending me there he bought me a brand new Honda 50cc motorcycle.

Before my mom left, neither Dad nor I knew what she was planning. One day, when Dad was at work, I came home from school, got the bread and peanut butter out, and opened the drawer to get a table knife to spread the peanut butter. There was a note in the drawer addressed to Dad. She wrote she was leaving him and that she had taken my siblings and some furniture with her. What? I had to go look because I hadn't noticed. Sure enough, there was no furniture in the living room and one of the three bedrooms was also void of furniture.

My reaction was immediate happiness. I was ecstatic and couldn't wait to tell Dad. I phoned him at work and said, "Guess what, Dad? Mom left, just you and me now."

His reaction was not one of happiness. All I heard was, "What?" followed by a long pause. So I read him the note. Dad and I lived alone in that house until Mom won it back in court. That took a year or two. I figured I had it made now. I didn't miss my siblings at all and really can't remember seeing any of them for years afterwards. I was quite happy living with Dad and he spoiled me rotten!

I was still in high school in grade ten when my folks split up. Shortly afterwards, I got into a fight with the biggest guy in my class, Marcus. He sat next to me and we often exchanged insults. I told him to meet me after class and we'd settle our differences outside. When a fight was announced there was always a big crowd that gathered to watch. Word of mouth could draw up to forty spectators.

I think I might have screwed up by challenging this giant. I nervously waited at the place commonly used for fighting, hoping he wouldn't show up so I wouldn't lose face. Ah crap! Here he comes and now I'm going to get the shit kicked out of me in front of all these kids.

Marcus came at me like a train at full speed. Oh-oh, I'm dead! He was running fast but I managed to side step him and kick him when he went by, although I almost fell. It slowed him down a bit, but he came at me again. He was expecting another kick, but this time I side stepped him again and hit him in the face with my elbow. He was bleeding and I was winning. My confidence was building, but surprisingly, that was it for him and he left.

Another fight I was in was with another known fighter, Jack. He was actually a good friend of mine. We chummed together a lot, but when I caught him flirting with my then-girlfriend at a party, I called him out. We had both been drinking, and he was sitting on the couch at the party repeatedly saying to me, "Friends to the end, friends to the end." He wasn't getting up so I went over and hit him in the face and gave him his first black eye. At least he said it was his first black eye when we hung around together afterward.

A few weeks later, we were out drinking in his dad's convertible with the top down. He had to piss so he turned into an alley blocking the sidewalk and pissed right there. Two adult couples were walking down the sidewalk and took issue with this behavior. They had been drinking too, so they were brave and told Jack to "move his fucking car".

Jack said, "Fuck you, Gramps. You are knee-high to a piston ring, so go home and go to bed." I got out of the car then because it looked like it was going to escalate from there. Luckily their wives coaxed them into moving on past Jack's jeers. Altercation avoided.

Because I had a motorcycle, I got a job at the local drug store delivering prescriptions year round. Didn't matter to me. While working there, I helped myself to chocolate bars and Playboy magazines when no one was watching. It was easy to do when you are an employee. No doubt about that.

I had two accidents with that motorcycle. The first was when I was out with my friend Gord, who also had a motorcycle. We were out riding one night when he waved at two people who were walking down the sidewalk. I looked over to see who they were. In that split-second of not paying attention, I ran into the back of a parked car. I had a helmet on that night because it was cold, but I was still knocked unconscious. I flew over the car and landed on my back. I hit the pavement so hard there was a dent on the back of my helmet. No injuries though. To this day I don't remember how my motorcycle and I got home.

Dad was fairly handy so we carried it down to the basement. He had to put on a new set of forks and a new front wheel. After he finished the repairs, he told me to give it a try across the rumpus room floor. I had about ten feet to stop, but there was a minor problem. I recognized that problem as soon as I applied the hand brake. He had forgotten to hook it up! I had my feet dangling down the sides so applying the foot brake wasn't an option because my reflexes weren't quick enough.

So when I applied the hand brake, nothing happened and I drove through the wall. Dad started swinging at me because apparently he thought it was my fault. I dropped the bike in his arms and took off out the door.

My second accident was on a busy highway. I was in a merge lane, trying to merge into traffic. A Volkswagen cut in front of me, and I ran into the side of it. Once again I flew over the top but this time, no helmet.

That resulted in my cheek and ear skidding across the pavement. That sanded off the outer layer of skin on the left side of my face. That time the motorcycle was fixed by the other driver's insurance because it wasn't my fault.

In those days, at fourteen years old, kids could legally obtain a license to drive a motorcycle, even with a passenger. We went everywhere we wanted to go on that bike.

I rarely bought gas because service stations closed before dusk in those days, and there was always gas left in the hoses once they turned the pumps off. I could drain at least four hoses at each station until I had enough gas to last a day or two. Sometimes I even filled the tank doing that. One time, I ran out of gas at Rick's house and couldn't find any gas cans. We did find some camp stove fuel in his dad's garage, so I put some in my tank hoping it would get me home. Damn! It worked and I made it home.

I almost got into trouble with the police while on that motorcycle. I was speeding and noticed a motorcycle cop coming up fast on me. He had a sidecar attached to his motorcycle, and it was pretty obvious he would not be able to split lanes to catch me. In other words, his "wider than normal" ride would not fit between two cars stopped at a red light and my Honda 50 would.

I was coming up on an intersection a block farther than my home because when I noticed the cop, I didn't turn down my street. The light ahead was red, and northbound traffic was two cars wide and about ten deep, and all were stopped at the light.

Perfect! I hardly slowed down and went right between the cars that were stopped at the light. I swung a hard right at the light on 50th Avenue and immediately made another hard right into a driveway just beyond the store on the corner. Behind that store was a dry cleaner with a drive-thru passageway that connected 50th Avenue to the alley between 50th and 51st Avenue. I went through the passageway and turned left in the alley, then up a block, took a right to my home alley and then I was at my house. My house was about three houses away from the street where I had left the cop and just behind where the cop first started chasing me. I pulled into my yard and covered my bike. My plan was flawlessly executed, and I got away clean.

My friend Rick and I used that motorcycle to take our .22 rifles out to a field on the outskirts of the city where we would shoot gophers all day. When driving out there, Rick had our .22 rifles strapped to his back while we motored down the highway. Or if we were going golfing, he had two sets of golf clubs, one set strapped to his back and the other pulled behind the motorcycle on a two-wheel golf pull cart. Never once did we get stopped by the police for carrying rifles or for pulling a trailer.

At the field, we competed to see who could shoot the most gophers. Somebody told us, that if you cut off their tails and took them to the zoo, they would pay 25 cents each for them. Initially, instead of shooting them, we trapped them because we thought if we cut off their tails and let them go, the tails would grow back, and we could catch them again. Once we found out that wasn't the case, we just shot them.

When hunting gophers, we quickly learned that once a gopher goes down a hole, if you wait long enough, nine times out of ten it will come back up that same hole. You just have to wait it out and then shoot when they poke their head up.

One day, I saw a great big animal go down a very large hole and I thought, Wow, I don't know what that is but I'm going to get it. I lay down right beside the hole with my rifle and aimed it where his head would come up, then waited for about fifteen minutes. It was a badger and the first one I'd ever seen. When it's head came up I shot, killing it instantly. Damn good thing too because I'm pretty sure that had I missed, it would've attacked me.

My buddy Rick was a half a mile down the field by the time I killed the badger. I had to show him my trophy so I carried it to him for bragging rights. That badger stunk so bad that I was gagging while running with it, trying everything to not puke. It was heavy, and the longer I held it, the heavier it seemed to get. I changed hands, often holding it off to the side so as not to inhale the stench that was blowing up my nostrils.

I think Rick was jealous because when I finally caught up to him, he didn't give me any whoop de do's. Instead, he told me that it was illegal to shoot badgers because they kill rodents and gophers. My triumph was short lived and on top of that, I had to ditch it somewhere so it wouldn't be found. Farmers always let us hunt gophers on their land because large animals can break a leg when stepping into a gopher hole. Killing the badger would not have been appreciated.

When trapping instead of shooting, we used leg-hold traps on the gophers, and they didn't require any bait. You just had to set them in the pathway of the hole you saw the animal go in. They were quite easy to catch because of that tendency to come out that same hole.

I tried to train one I caught in a trap. I made a leash out of a thin rope and took it to school. It bit me a couple of times when I handled it, but I generated a lot of attention from the kids at school. Eventually it got off the leash and ran away.

I used to catch pigeons too, and I wanted to keep two really nice pigeons as pets in my bedroom. I had a wire cage that was about three feet square. I brought it down to my bedroom to put the pigeons in when I went to school. When I returned home after school, I realized what a stupid idea that was. For some reason I didn't notice the wire cage spacing was wide enough for the pigeons to get out. My room was a disaster. There was pigeon shit everywhere – on the walls, on my bed, on the floor, everywhere! It took a little while to catch them again in the bedroom, but once I did, I just took them outside and let them go. Then I took the cage back outside and spent the next few hours cleaning up pigeon shit.

Where we learned to catch our pigeons was in a dangerous place. We were only fourteen years old at the time. The dam provided power for the city we lived in, as do most dams in most cities. We saw some kids coming out of a room on the underside of the road one day so we investigated. They had two rooms beneath the road, one on either side of it. To get to the rooms, we had to shimmy along a one-foot-wide concrete walkway above the water on one side and with a drop-off on the other.

The rooms had dirt floors that sloped up towards the road. At any given time of day, these rooms were filled with pigeons. There was some chicken wire screening in the room that we usually entered. Workers might have put it there to cover the entrance so the pigeons couldn't get in.

We took burlap sacks with us and crawled up to the top of the sloped dirt where lots of pigeons were nestled into the corner. We just had to grab them and put them in the sacks. Later in life, I learned that pigeon excrement can carry some very dangerous bacteria and that room was probably quite contaminated.

When we had enough birds, we took them to a Chinese restaurant a mile or so away and sold them to the owner for 25 cents, or sometimes 50 cents depending on the quality and quantity. I don't know how you feel about Chinese food but for some reason, I just don't have a taste for it.

My buddy Gord and I later got jobs at a large grocery chain. We cleaned produce racks after the store was closed. We were always looking for ways to make extra money, and we had easy access to cigarettes in that store. There were only a few employees, all adults, working there at night, but they were too busy stocking shelves which left us unsupervised.

We were able to get cigarette packages out of the store by lifting one of the delivery doors at the back. They were locked closed, but they could be pulled up about an inch before the locked chain stopped them from opening further. Maybe they suspected we were taking stuff because when we were leaving after our shift one night, the guy standing at the door to let us out jokingly asked if we had stolen anything. We laughed it off and later, after all the adults went home, we recovered the cigarettes on the ground outside the roll-up door. We sold them to friends at school or to anyone with money.

We also sold condoms that we pilfered from a nearby drug store. A lot of the guys wanted condoms for bragging rights, but seeing the round wear marks in their wallets was an indicator the condoms were more for show than for their intended purpose. I enjoyed my life very much, and I think Dad did too. During that time, he threw a party and invited quite a few people. I chose to stay in my downstairs bedroom during the party because I had plans to go out the window to meet friends. I figured that would be a better option for me to have a good time without anyone missing me.

My buddy Terry knocked on my window and then waited for me to come out. I tried to open it, but the outside storm window was stuck, and we were unable to get it open. I signaled for Terry to stand back because I had an idea. I used the butt end of my .22 rifle to smash the glass. As it happened, one of Dad's guests was out on the back steps smoking and heard the glass break.

He came running around the corner to investigate and saw my buddy standing there. As soon as Terry saw him he ran off. The chase was on, but Terry was fast and he got away. The guest came back and looked in the window through the broken glass and said, "What is going on?"

I looked at him with a confused look and said, "I don't know. I was sleeping and I think somebody tried to break in." He thought he had saved the day, but if you really think about it, he should have noticed that the broken glass was on the outside of the window, not on the inside. Most houses back then had single-pane windows inside and storm windows on the outside. The inside window wasn't the problem, but the storm window was nailed in place. No wonder we couldn't get it open.

Once I cleaned up the glass, I waited until things calmed down and then left through that window to join my friends at a designated meeting spot. Dad never even knew I was gone that night because upon returning, I re-entered my bedroom the same way that I had left. The guy that chased Terry told my dad about the attempted break-in so Dad put a new glass in the next day.

One day, I didn't really feel like going to school, so when Dad came to wake me up, I opened my bedroom door and said, "I can't go to school today because I feel really sick and I puked on the floor last night."

I pointed to the vomit on the floor. He didn't realize that the night before I had made that vomit up in a cup. I made it with a little mustard, some milk, a few beans, and whatever else I found to make it look like puke. While I was mixing it, Dad had come into the kitchen and said, "What are you doing?"

I had the cup in my hand and I was stirring it with a spoon so I said, "Just making myself a snack." Then I put a spoonful in my mouth. It was horrible tasting, but it was better than foiling my excuse for missing school the next day. The next morning, he believed that I had thrown up and told me to clean it up sometime during the day. I did, but what a job that was. It was a sticky, hardened mixture by the time I got to it.

I stole my first car at fourteen years old simply for joy riding. My friend Pete and I would check local service stations for cars with keys in them. We'd drive them around but would always return them to where we got them.

We once took a 1956 Oldsmobile and picked up a hitchhiker. We asked him how he liked the car. He said, "It's nice." I wanted to freak him out a bit so I said, "It's stolen." We all laughed, but Pete and I were laughing more because saying that seemed to rattle the kid. He asked us to drop him off right afterwards. My erratic driving might have also contributed to his wanting to get out of the car early. We didn't worry too much about getting caught because we knew that juveniles who commit criminal offenses can be charged under the criminal code but do not carry that conviction into their adult life. Not having a driver's license isn't a criminal offense. However, I did have a license to drive a motorcycle. We could have been charged back then with what was called 'joy riding' and it was a joy!

Another car I stole belonged to Dad's girlfriend. I found it parked in our garage. I was checking to see if Dad's car was in there and was surprised to find a nice 1952 Chev parked there. Bonus! Now, I could drive to the school basketball game. It had no keys in it, but I hot wired it, took the car and drove the shit out of it, eventually overheating the engine. I released the radiator cap to cool it down faster, but that created a volcano of anti freeze all over the fenders and windshield.

Stupid me, I should have cleaned it all up before I parked it back in the garage, but I didn't. When Dad and his lady returned, they knew right away that someone had driven that car and that someone was me. Dad made me go meet his new girlfriend to apologize to her and told me to clean the car up while I was over there. I apologized but she said she'd look after the cleaning.

I clued in right away that she was very interested in my dad, so I took advantage of that. I asked to borrow her car to go out on a date with a girl. I just got my driver's license so she was a bit concerned about my driving experience.

However, she let me use the car. Big mistake! I didn't have a date yet, but picked up my friend Bruce and we got a guy at the liquor store to buy us beer. That was all we needed to entice a couple of nice-looking girls to accompany us.

One of them sat in the back with Bruce, and the other sat in the front with me. We drank a lot of beer, and I was quite intoxicated to say the least. In fact I was so drunk that with my limited experience in a car, I tried to make a right hand turn onto a busy street before an oncoming car reached me.

I failed to let go of the steering wheel and made a 180-degree turn into a telephone pole. It broke off and fell over, blocking three out of four lanes on that busy road. I put my teeth through my bottom lip when my face smacked into the steering wheel. Bruce and his date flew forward against the front seat, bending it straight up from its sloped position. The two girls jumped out and took off, and Bruce and I were taken to hospital by ambulance. The cops showed up at the hospital and asked us who was in the car with us. We insisted it was just the two of us. They knew we were lying but didn't pursue it any further. I was so lucky they chose not to move any further on it.

Dad's girlfriend's car was a write-off. She really liked Dad a lot, and they later married, much later! She didn't seem to hold any grudges against me, which was odd, so I assume she sensed my dad and I were very close and she didn't want to disturb the waters in that pool. She was actually a very nice person and in the thirty plus years she was married to Dad, we always got along very well.

I used to take Dad's car (without his knowledge) for joy rides on occasion as well. One night, I took it and picked up three of my friends to go joy riding. My dad was at a party at my uncle's, and I knew they partied downstairs in the basement while their booze and mix were upstairs in the kitchen. When someone needed a drink they came upstairs to get it.

My friends and I went there, and I parked and waited outside the front door where I had a clear view of the kitchen. All the booze was out on the counter. As soon as someone from the party left the kitchen with a fresh drink, I quickly went in and scooped a full bottle of Scotch. We passed it around in the car, each taking a sip, and on my turn, I took a guzzle.

I got so drunk that my friend Gord had to drive the car. I sat in the back seat, and he drove everyone home, including me, and then walked home. However, before anyone went home, I had to pee. Gord pulled into a parking lot and I got out. While in midstream someone yelled, "COPS!" I panicked and jumped back into the car while still pissing. I peed all over the back of the front seat and the seat I was sitting in. Nobody got wet but me. They were lucky!

In the morning, Dad woke me up and said, "You took my car last night, didn't you."

I knew better than to lie to him, so I said, "Yes, I did."

Then he said, "And you spilled pop all over the inside."

Okay, I might have to lie there! I said, "Yes, I did. I'm sorry!" Whew, that was close! I never even got grounded.

Then Dad bought me a 1955 Dodge Mayfair with loud pipes, a stick shift, and a 272 Red Ram V8 Hemi engine. It even had spinner hubcaps with naked ladies attached to them. Dad was sure good to me.

The A&W was the "go to" place for teens. Often times, three of us would go there for a root beer or a burger but mostly just to check out the girl situation. With bench seats back then, all three of us sat in the front. One day, I was riding as a passenger in Rick's car with Don. Of course, Rick was driving. I lost the toss and had to sit in the middle. The guy in the middle always needed to be alert because if the guy on the passenger side bends down to pretend to tie his shoe, and the guy in the middle doesn't notice, it makes the driver and the guy in the middle look like they're out on a date because they're sitting so close to each other. No one can see the guy that has ducked down pretending to tie his shoes. The only way to avoid any embarrassment was for the guy in the middle to duck down as well so only the driver is visible from the outside. Then it's a standoff to see who has the most stamina and can stay down the longest.

Another thing that all the guys did at the A&W was to engage in sonic drags. That's basically a competition to see who has the loudest pipes while parked. You simply rev your engine to get the rumble out the back, and the car that had the loudest pipes was the winner of the sonic drags that day. No trophies and no clear winners, just noise.

Going through the A&W parking lot, you had to burn rubber (of course) to impress anybody that was watching.

You would come to a stop first, and then pop the clutch and let the tires scream. Sometimes black smoke would be coming out the back from the rubber burning. One time, I went through the A&W first without burning rubber to get myself a milkshake, then I went back around to do the burnouts. Like an idiot, I had my milkshake sitting up on the dashboard, so when I popped the clutch, I launched the milkshake off the dashboard and onto my lap. That was the end of that day because I had to go home and change. I only hoped that nobody saw what happened and I sure as hell wasn't going to tell anybody.

It wasn't long before I crashed that vehicle. I went to the lake with Bruce. We picked up a couple of girls and took them to a drive-in theatre. We did a lot of drinking, so on the drive back to the lake, I fell asleep at highway speed and drove through nine fence posts strung with barbed wire and my second telephone pole. That pole had about a hundred phone and electrical wires attached to it. The top part of the pole was still dangling from the wires, which were all still intact. The bottom part was shrapnel.

Thankfully, none of us were injured. The four of us hitchhiked back to the lake where the girls were staying, and we spent the night with them. When we got there, I phoned the police and they told me that I should get the car out of there ASAP because it was in a bad area. If I didn't salvage it before daylight, there wouldn't be many parts left on it.

In the morning, Bruce and I went back and got the car out of that tangled mess of barbed wire. The windshield was separated from the roof, leaving an inch of space so that cold air could blow into the car. The floorboards were pushed up about three inches, but I could still operate the pedals. The back wheel was bent so it wobbled, but I drove it like that all the way home.

Before we left the lake, I phoned Dad and told him that I had totaled the car. He got pretty angry and said, "Get home right now!"

I neglected to tell him that we were a couple of hundred miles away, so he was expecting me to come home a lot sooner than I did. I didn't get home until late in the evening because we couldn't go very fast. The car was shaking so bad that it felt like I was on a carnival ride. There was no amount of fixing that could make that car roadworthy again. It was a total write-off.

You might expect that I was a handful at school as well. Perhaps, I might have been a little difficult. While in my first year of high school, my buddies and I entertained ourselves by chewing paper and making spit balls. We then threw them at the clock high up on the wall.

Someone told me that if I put a wet spitball into a light socket after turning off the switch and then screwed the bulb back in, it would explode when someone turned the switch back on. I thought I'd give it a try.

My teacher at that time was a very weird individual who put lots of holding agent in his hair to make two perfect little curls right at the front of his hairline. It looked ridiculous. Anyway, he entered the room just in time to catch me standing on a desk unscrewing a light bulb with chewed-up paper in my mouth. I didn't see him come in, and he quickly walked up to me and punched me in the stomach. Surprised that he had done that, I jumped off the desk and shoved him against the wall. It seemed to shake him a bit, so he told me to go to the principal's office and tell the principal I had pushed him.

I said, "Sure, but you come with me and tell him you punched me in the stomach."

Then he said, "Just go sit down at your desk."

This same teacher (with the two weird circles of hair) bumped into me years later when I was walking a beat as a cop. He seemed shocked that I had become a cop and initiated a stupid conversation. He said, "What are you doing these days, Dick?" Now you see why it was stupid conversation. I was standing in front of him in a police uniform while on duty, and this was the best he could come up with?

I was tempted to say, "What the fuck do you think I'm doing you two-curled moron? Can't you see how I'm dressed?" However, I chose diplomacy and said, "As you can see, I've joined the police department." Then we had a meaningless chat and went on our separate ways. We were probably both thinking the same thing: "What an asshole!"

When I was still in grade ten, Dad had an opportunity to move to another city 400 miles away to be an insurance broker representing the company he had been working for, but now he would be his own boss. His girlfriend didn't want to live too far away from him, so she eventually moved there and rented a house right across the street from the house Dad had rented.

When we moved to that smaller city, I transferred to a school there to continue my education. However, before we moved I had already been skipping most of my classes to hang out at the local pool hall, so after we moved I just continued that trend.

It was a few months before Dad learned that I was not attending school. He found out because one of my new teachers lived right next door and he and Dad became friends. Since the cat was out of the bag that I had no interest in continuing my education, I got a job at a small catalogue store. I worked in the automotive department. They didn't pay very well – just $50 a week plus commission. I pilfered a lot of stuff at that small catalogue department store. I'd hide it out on the loading dock at the back and pick it up after the store closed and everyone had gone home. That's how I got my "booty" out undetected.

Between three and six months after Dad's girlfriend moved there, she began working at a large department store as a secretary for one of the section managers. Eventually she asked me if I wanted to work there because the pay was fifteen dollars a week more. I took the opportunity because I figured I could still supplement my income one way or another.

As it turned out, I never did take anything from that store because I didn't want to embarrass her or Dad. I also pumped gas at this job because I worked in the automotive department and they had gas pumps on site. I could make an extra dollar or two by checking someone's oil and telling them that it was down a quart when it wasn't. Most people paid in cash at that time because credit cards weren't used like they are today and most people did not ask for a receipt after they paid. That meant I was able to put the money for gas into the till but hold back the amount I collected for the quart of oil that wasn't put in the car.

Oil cans used to be poured using metal spouts that you stabbed or pierced the can with to funnel the oil into the motor. To fool the owner of the car, I kept an empty can of oil on the rack with the full ones. I pretended to pierce the can by pushing the funnel spout back into the hole that was already there. Then I turned the can upside down into their engine. They thought I was topping up the oil when I wasn't. Next I'd check the dipstick again and tell them their oil was good now. Not even one of the customers caught on, so I did all right.

One Halloween a buddy showed up. We were thinking about something to do, and he suggested we go to his house and get some eggs and do some egg throwing.

There was an old wooden bridge in our town that had replaced a new bridge that paralleled it. The old bridge stayed in place for quite a long time after the new one was built. As we were walking across the old bridge, we were approached by a security guard who was guarding it for Halloween. He asked where we were going and what we were up to.

I had a brain lapse and said, "We are just on our way to Chuck's house. It's just on the other side. We're going to get some eggs, and then we're going to come back here and throw them at you." We all had a good laugh over that, and then we went on our way to Chuck's house. We got some eggs and came back and threw them at him. It seemed quite funny to us, but probably not to him.

Dad took in a couple of roommates to supplement the rent and one of them was a jerk. His name was Wayne. He was a nerd but he had quite a collection of skin books and Playboy magazines that he kept in his room. Of course, I helped myself to those whenever he wasn't home, but he eventually found out. He confronted me about going in his room, and I told him to go screw himself. He took a swing at me, but I grabbed him by the arm and threw him into the bathroom. He fell into the tub and gave up right away.

He tried to talk Dad into kicking me out of the house because I had assaulted him. Dad said, "If anybody's going to leave, Wayne, it's going to be you, not my son." Wayne left. We still had Duncan as a roommate, but he was a good guy and easy to get along with.

Once evening rolled around and the end of the work day had passed, Dad would almost always let me use his car while he walked across the street to visit his girlfriend.

His car was a 1964 Meteor with a pretty zippy 352 engine in it. When I was working in the automotive section of the catalogue store, I had taken a set of baby moon hubcaps just to use whenever I borrowed Dad's car in order to make it look like it was mine. Then I would cruise the strip in town looking to race with others or drive by the local Dairy Queen or A&W, and burn rubber to try and impress any girls that were watching.

It was a good time back in those days. I almost always had a friend or two with me in the car, and we always had booze. One day, I dropped off my friend Howard at his house and was on my way back home when a guy pulled up beside me on the bridge and asked if I wanted to race him.

I couldn't turn down his request, so we raced and I beat his ass. He caught up to me and pulled me over and said, "Hey, you want a beer?" Sure, I thought. I was out of beer so figured I might be able to score a few more.

I got into his car and left Dad's car parked on the side of the road with the windows down. Then the guy told me there was a party going on a few blocks away and invited me. Ah, more beer! "Okay." So we drove off in his car to the party. It turned out this guy belonged to an outlaw motorcycle club called the Devil's Escorts.

Traditionally, when an outlaw motorcycle club member invites you to a party, it can be a preliminary gesture to get the other members to size you up before allowing you to "hang around" with them. After a period of time, probably a year or so, you might be invited to be a "prospect" for an undetermined period of time before a vote can be made to "patch you in" as a full member. That could take another year or more.

Is this where my life was taking me? Into the outlaw motorcycle world? I'm quite sure I would have joined if I was asked to be a "hang around", but it was not meant to be! My dad was about to pull the pin on that! The picture below is a modified copy of a newspaper article. I modified it to remove identification of police agency, location, and names.

Eleven youth's appeared in court as a result of involvement in weekend incidents in which two officers being injured and four others attacked. Twenty charges were laid ranging from assault of a police officer causing bodily harm, creating a disturbance and wilful property damage. A local gang known as the Devils Escorts in sleeveless denim with gang identification patches were involved after one of their members kicked in a window of a private vehicle.

The party was close to the river where construction was happening, so barricades blocked the road to the location. There were about fifteen bikers there with their women, and they welcomed me after being introduced by the guy who had brought me there.

Meanwhile the cops noticed Dad's car parked with the windows down and thought it was stolen because people don't usually leave their windows down at night in the rain. (It wasn't raining when I left it.) They called Dad to see if he knew where his car was. He said his son had it. They told him there was a party going on by the river, so he might want to check and see if I was there.

Dad got his girlfriend to drive him to the car and used his spare keys to take his car to try and find me. He eventually found the party and got out of his car to yell at me to get in the car. That was embarrassing! Now these guys know that my nice new car with my stolen baby moon hubcaps was actually "Daddy's car", not mine, and "Daddy" was here to bring me home.

I immediately lost any respect I may have gained from those guys when I joined the party. I thought, Holy shit! Dad and I could both get the crap kicked out of us if I don't act fast. So, as embarrassing as it was, I left with him. When we got home, he swung at me, but I grabbed his arm, gave him a glance and said, "You won't be doing that."

I truly love my dad and always have, but with a little liquor in me, I disappointed and sometimes scared him. If life had taken me into the outlaw motorcycle world, it would have been great because I loved to fight and I loved to party. I feel I might have excelled as the bad ass I always imagined.

I was still living with my dad and driving his car, but it was sometimes difficult to find enough money to put gas back in it. The solution for that was to secure a gas can and a syphon hose and then drive around the neighborhood looking for isolated vehicles from which to syphon gasoline.

Once we spotted a potential donor, we parked a block away and walked back to the target vehicle. This of course was done after the sun went down to make it more difficult for anyone to see us. After we had filled the gas can and were returning to Dad's car parked a block away, we saw there was a police car parked right behind us. Holy shit! Someone must have seen us and reported us to the police.

The strategy was to wait the cop out, and as soon as he left, we would get in the car and skedaddle out of there. A couple of hours went by and the cop wasn't giving up, so we needed to change that strategy. We hid the syphon hose and gas can full of gas behind some garbage cans. Then we boldly returned to the car armed with the excuse that we had parked there and visited some girls. We couldn't park at their house because their parents were not aware we were visiting the girls. That should work!

As soon as we got close enough to the cop we were delighted to discover there was no one in the police car. He was either visiting a lady at the residence where he parked or he lived there. Damn! We wasted almost three hours to discover that! We drove back to recover our stolen gas, put it in our tank, and then went home because our evening was now over.

We used to attend events held in the park in the downtown area just to look for fights. One night I got into one. Somehow, I injured my opponent, probably with my ring, but it looked like I had stabbed him with a fork. From the rumors I heard afterwards, people were saying I did use a fork and I was being called a psycho. Wow! My reputation was spreading. Some would consider that to be a bad thing. I found it rather complimentary.

Dad's boat had a 65HP Mercury outboard on it that he quite often let me take to the lake with my buddies. We'd take a tent along and camp there for the weekend and use the boat for a good time and to attract girls. On one occasion, one of my buddies was driving the boat and I was waterskiing off the back. I told him to come in close to shore so I could swoop in and turn my skis in sharply to make an impressive stop at the shoreline. Then I planned to strut off like a true athlete.

That didn't work out so well because I came in much too fast. I couldn't turn the skis. They stuck in the sand and I went ass over tea-kettle up the beach in front of a whole bunch of girls. There goes my psycho reputation; my athlete dream was not meant to be. It did get some laughter though. It was quite embarrassing and was one of those moments you just never forget. My back got all cut up and scratched to remind me that I was not the skier that I thought I was.

Another night, I borrowed Dad's car and picked up my buddies. We went on to the sandbar alongside the river, and I was driving like an idiot again. I ended up getting stuck and the car was buried right down to the rocker panels in the sand. So my friends and I went out looking for planks. The plan was to jack the car up and drive it over the planks in the sand, eight feet at a time. That's if we could find some eight-foot planks. We did find some at a construction site and took four of them.

We used them under the front and back wheels of the car over and over again, putting one plank under each wheel every eight feet. It meant jacking up the car and putting planks under each wheel for every eight feet of travel. We did get it out of the sand, but it took several hours to move about fifty feet. It was slow, tedious, and time consuming.

I then dropped my buddies off, but when I was going home I looked at the odometer. It had just turned over to a number with way too many zeros behind it. Since there were so many zeros showing, I was sure my dad would notice that the mileage was considerably higher than he might have expected. To get it back down, I drove backwards for about thirty minutes until the odometer registered in the high nines without too many repetitive numbers in a row. All those zeros were no longer an issue.

In the future, I disconnected the speedometer cable. The lease company had put a copper wire seal on it to prevent that, but I was able to pull the copper wire back through the squashed lead. I only made the loop large enough to get the cable end through so the leasing company would think it had just been installed improperly.

I used to hold my foot on the brake and apply the gas at the same time and then ease off on the brake until the rear wheel started spinning, I could make a "rubber cloud of black smoke" that was huge. That was just part of the fun we had when cruising the strip, especially when you didn't own the car you were driving the shit out of.

I only worked at the same place as my dad's girlfriend for a few months when she told me the store had strict nepotism regulations and they were talking about getting married, so once they tied the knot, one of us had to resign. I was ready to get out on my own anyway, so I said I would take the hit when the time comes. Then the day came! I was best man at a six person wedding at city hall. I was happy for my dad. I got along great with her too which is a good thing. So, now that she was my stepmother, I had to quit because of the 'alleged' nepotism. I say 'alleged' because I'm not stupid. Good move on her part though! Hell, I was a third wheel in their relationship anyway. I was seventeen years old and now I have another opportunity to seek out a new path in life.

Part Four:
Out on My Own

THE DAY I left home I caught a ride back to my hometown with a guy I used to work with. I stayed with him and the family he was visiting for one night, and then called one of my old pals to see if they could put me up until I got a job. He checked with his parents, and they allowed me to sleep in the basement on an old bed they had set up down there. His parents were deaf mutes so noise was not an issue. What was an issue were vibrations. My buddy and I went out at night to party, but his parents expected him home at a decent hour. We ignored the curfew and returned back to his place at about 2:00 a.m. unconcerned that his deaf parents would catch us. We knew they would be sound asleep by then. WRONG! We woke them up because of the vibrations we created when sneaking in. Yes, vibrations! Their senses in that respect were like 'super powers' and we were busted. I knew I was causing problems in their family just being there because

I could feel the tension. They didn't ask me to leave, but I thought it would be best to do so.

I got a job at the pizza joint where I used to hang out when I was still in high school. I became good friends with one of guys that I worked with most of the time. After a few months, the owner of the pizza joint decided to open up a second pizza joint in a tourist area in another city. He asked us if we wanted to go there and work for him. That sounded like a good idea, so why not? While working there I had an unruly customer who didn't seem to like the way the pizza was made and wanted another one to replace it. It appeared he was showing off to his friends because they had already ate half their pizza.

"No problem," I said. "Just give me a few minutes, and I'll bring it out to you." I found a big, ugly, hairy spider in the corner in the back room, so I caught it and used it in the base of the pizza. I covered it with tomato sauce, cheese, and all the ingredients he wanted. I hope those guys enjoyed it because I sure as hell enjoyed watching them eat it.

This new pizza joint that was over 400 miles away. My buddy, Colin only had a $50 car so we anticipated there might be some mechanical issues with it on the way there. In fact we did have trouble because the transmission lost first and reverse gears. It was a standard transmission, so it was no big deal to change it, but where were we going to get one?

Lo and behold there was a compatible donor on a car lot on one of the corners in town. I only weighed about 145 pounds at that time, and I managed to get underneath to unbolt the driveshaft. I was about to start on the transmission when a cop car stopped at the corner for a red light not more than thirty feet from the car I was lying under. It was almost dark but had he been paying attention he might have seen me. I kept calm but was thinking, Shit! Can he see me here?

Luckily he didn't, but it was enough of a scare that I got the hell out of there and left the car somewhat incapacitated with the driveshaft lying under it. I could easily have taken it, but we didn't need a driveshaft. So we just drove Colin's car without first or reverse gears. We had to make sure that when we stopped we didn't have to back up, and we could still drive it forward by starting in second gear. Starting in second gear was very hard on the clutch, so before too long it gave out and rendered the car useless.

Our wages were low at best for making pizzas and were not enough to make a living, so we camped in our tent on the lake shoreline. We almost never had to buy groceries because we used to trade pizza for fried chicken at the chicken place next door to our pizza joint.

The one big problem with tent living was earwigs. There were so many earwigs in there that we chose to sleep outside or in the car, even when it rained. My buddy got a little liquored up one night, and I found him sitting on the floor of the tent wearing only his underwear. He had a shoe in his hand that he was using to whack any earwigs within his reach. Too funny. If we only had iPhones back then. He was overweight and had on white underwear that looked like a diaper, so to me he looked like a fat Buddha trying to catch cockroaches and losing the battle.

Of course when you are living in a tent, it means that when you are away at work or wherever, the tent is left abandoned. Therefore, it was subject to invasion by others. Anything that we didn't need that particular day we left behind in the tent. We even had a stash of money in there, but we hid it so it wasn't in plain sight. I'm not sure whether we were just brain dead or drunk, but somehow we thought that it would be a good idea to hide our money inside a lantern. Someone did enter our tent and took what they deemed to be valuable, which included our lantern. Duh!

While in that tourist city, we met some girls who lived up the hill above the lake from where we were camping. Three of us were drinking beer at the home of one of them one night. When my buddies and I left their place, we walked a couple of miles down the switchback roadway carrying our leftover beers and smashing the empties on the road. Of course, someone called the cops and reported that three boys were smashing beer bottles. Meanwhile, Colin had to pee, so he said he would pee in the bush and then take a short cut to the next road down on the switchback.

He disappeared into the bush. Within seconds, a cop car pulled us over and had us in the back seat of the police cruiser. The cop accused us of smashing bottles on the road because someone reported three guys doing just that. "Couldn't be us, sir. There are only two of us," we said.

At that point, Colin had seen the car and could hear us talking, but he didn't notice it was a cop car. He knew we had gotten in the car. He thought we just waved it down to get a ride, so he ran down to the next section of road on the switchback to intercept us. He was still unaware it was a police car.

We had just convinced the cop that it wasn't us smashing bottles when Colin jumped out on the road as the bright lights of the cop car approached him. He waved us down. By the time he noticed it was a cop car, the gig was up. The first thing he said to us was, "Looks like they caught you guys."

I was thinking, Colin, you dummy! You just let the cop know he caught the right guys.

We were originally under the impression that the cop was going to drop us off at the bottom of the hill close to our tent. Instead, he took us to the police station. He did not charge us with anything, but he recorded all of our names and birth dates and told us we had 24 hours to get our stuff at the lake and get out of town. Sounds like the Wild West, but it really happened. I couldn't believe my ears! I ignored his stupid request. The other two left for the big city.

It wasn't too long before I had a girlfriend who lived in town, and her folks let me pitch the tent in their backyard. I caught the biggest, ugliest white spider while in my tent.

I had it in a mason jar and showed my girlfriend and her mother. I hate spiders and didn't want to sleep in my tent any more, so my girlfriend's mother put a cot in the front porch and let me sleep there.

Colin had already gone back to the big city, but I decided to stay because I now had more interest in this town. My girlfriend's parents encouraged me to go back to school to finish my high school. I had only gone part way through grade ten in school, so it seemed like something I might want to try. Try is about all I did, and I did not try very hard, so a month or so later I quit.

I did find it quite interesting, however, that in the few weeks I was in school, I seemed to be more popular than I remembered when I previously went to school. I chalked that up to the fact that I was probably more interesting to people because I wasn't someone who lived at home. For some reason or another that made me more interesting to girls. The guys, however, not so much!

I bought a pretty nice 1955 Chevy two-door sedan while I was there for only $50. Car insurance wasn't something people really had to buy in those days, so all I had to do was put a license plate on, it and I was good to go. It wasn't long before the girlfriend's mother told me I had to leave anyway. She got a little hot under the collar because I was living rent-free and eating their groceries. I never even thought about that but, yah, I would have thrown me out too!

My buddy Lloyd asked me if I was interested in going up north to paint railroad bridges. He said I didn't need any money because food and lodging were supplied by his dad, who would be my new employer. I agreed, so the next day, we headed out with his dad to a small town where I was put up in a hotel for a few weeks while we were working. My meal costs were covered along with my room charges.

The next morning, we headed out to an old steel railroad bridge way back in the bush. While on route to paint the bridge, the roads were so muddy that we got stuck axle deep. We had passed by a grader that was parked on the side of the road about a mile back, so Lloyd and I walked back to see if it had keys in it. If it did, we could use it to pull ourselves out of the mud. But first, we'd have to figure out how to operate it.

We were lucky the keys were in it, so we fiddled with it for a while until we could get it to do what we wanted. Then we drove it back and pulled the car out with a chain that was in the cab. The operator must have freaked out when he returned to where his machine was so hopefully he was able to follow the tracks to where we left it.

That job was tough because I had to hang from a harness to sandblast the bridge straddling the river. Our equipment was sub-standard, and my boss was a crook. We almost had to beg him for the wages he owed us. Then he'd cheat us on our time. A couple of weeks later, we went back to paint commercial buildings. I stayed at Lloyd's place while we painted a bakery. I didn't mind the outdoor work, but painting buildings was monotonous, so I quit. Lloyd's dad wouldn't pay me, so now I was broke and didn't have a place to stay.

At seventeen, I experienced homelessness for the first time in my life. I needed to find a commercial building that had easy access to the roof and I knew just the place so I camped up there for about a week. The building was the pizza joint I had previously worked for, and I still knew the people who were working there. They helped me out with free pizza when I was hungry but had no idea I was living on the roof.

One day when I was bullshitting with one of my friends, (Norm), I talked him into breaking into the place that night. We broke in through a small window at the back of the building. Once inside, we broke into the jukebox to get the money out. We even made a pizza. I knew the layout well, having worked there before. The kitchen was completely visible from the outside because it had a huge storefront window. While we were making the pizza, a beat cop walked by and saw us.

This pizza joint was on his beat and cops walked by it all the time. On this occasion, we kept the lights on to make it look like we were staff members cleaning up. I waved at him just like I did when I worked there, anticipating he would view us as employees. He waved back and kept walking. That put us at ease. Had he not seen us, he might have walked around to check the back of the building and discovered the broken window. What a relief! I almost shit myself.

Then a couple of days later, a different beat cop saw me climbing up onto the roof and called for me to come down. I explained to him that I had no job, no money, and no place to go. I said I only needed a few more days to find a job so I could get a room somewhere. Surprisingly, he took me under his wing and let me stay at his place for a few weeks. That policeman had a huge influence on my decision to join the police department later on in life. The irony is that after I became a policeman, he got fired for stealing from the property room at police headquarters.

Later, in my four years on the police department, I learned that corruption was expected but getting caught wasn't.

I got a job right away at an electrical equipment wholesale place. I rented a one-room apartment a few blocks from my new place of employment. I was their new delivery driver. I encouraged two friends, Gord and Rick, to apply for job openings there as order pickers, and they were hired.

They picked items ordered by customers, wrapped them for delivery, and numbered the parcels. We set up a system where they would include an extra package or two with any random order and mark those stolen packages with a circled number. The packages included blenders, toasters, waffle irons, and many other small appliances. Sometimes extra packages were included in two or three different orders, all placed in my truck. The circled number on the stolen package was hardly noticeable by others, but I could easily identify them. I dropped them off at my apartment before starting my deliveries. It was a great system; nobody got caught and the profits were outstanding.

I soon moved into an apartment complex with a couple of friends, Gerry and Matt. Our apartment was on the sixth floor. Then I quit the job at the electrical wholesalers and went to work as a banquet set-up employee. I set up banquet rooms at weddings and such, and I drove the delivery step van from the caterers to the banquet.

We catered mostly to impressive weddings. The banquet rooms were always top of the line with new, crisp-looking, fancy linen on all the tables. The food was always very plentiful. My catering truck had slots for two-feet by three-feet metal trays that were artistically decorated with food. It was always presented in expensive-looking patterns.

There were meats, cheeses, breads, vegetables, and multiple trays of desserts. When the banquet ended, I picked up all the dishes and leftover food. On the trip back to the restaurant I would drop off a few trays at our apartment and some were actually untouched. The food bill for the three of us was pretty much nil. We ate well. That meant more money for booze.

That apartment building had balconies for every suite and the balconies had iron railings to prevent people from falling off. We used to have fun racing each other. One would go down the outside of the balconies, and one would run down the stairs or take the elevator. The first guy to make it to the back parking lot won the bet. Luckily none of us fell or even came close to falling. Personally I went down the outside railings several times during the time we lived in that apartment building.

Once in awhile I would come face-to-face with occupants of the suites below us glancing out of their glass patio doors. It did generate complaints from time to time, and the live-in caretaker would knock on our door. That usually ended in a confrontation and threats against him.

Occasionally one of us would even chase him down the hall, and he would run down the stairs to escape. One day, two of my roommates were wrestling on the living room floor. One flipped the other over, and his foot went through the glass on the patio door. It was not safety glass because it didn't shatter, but there was a one-and-a-half-foot hole in the bottom-right corner. The glass had to be replaced, so we had to report it. This resulted in us being kicked out of that place.

I then moved into a motel with one of my roommates. One night, when I returned to our room, there was a party going on. I was not made aware that there was going to be a party, so I was quite angry and I told everybody to get the hell out! The response appeared to be taken too lightly because my demand was laughed off. There was an ironing board set up in the room with an iron still on it. It was beside some liquor bottles so I picked up an empty bottle and smashed it against the iron, exposing the jagged broken edges. That got everyone's' attention. Then I blurted out in a more aggressive tone for everybody to leave. My demeanor elevated to "crazy man" and everyone left immediately. I was happy with the results!

I was always quick to fight, so they took my threat seriously. I used to pick fights just for entertainment. One time in the pizza joint, there was a table with four guys at it. I went over and put my hand on top of the entire pizza and insulted them. That should have resulted in a fight, but they didn't seem to want to deal with me so I moved on. I probably was too drunk to fight anyway considering the odds.

I didn't always win my fights, but I often did. Losing has the advantage of teaching you where you went wrong. One time a guy pulled a knife on me. When I saw the knife in his hand, I kicked him and the knife blade folded onto his finger and cut him. He dropped the knife and ran for the door, but he missed the push bar when going out and hit the glass with his hands and foot, busting the glass out of it. That one was safety glass because it shattered.

That guy had arrived on a motorcycle that was parked around back on a long driveway that went out to the street. He wasn't having a good day because he did a wheelie to try to impress us when he was leaving, but he lost control of his motorcycle and wiped out on the driveway. It was very humiliating for him because by that time there were half a dozen people out there watching his performance and laughing at the crash.

Another fight was at a place where people my age 17-19, some a little older and some a little younger. There was a guy parked in his car alongside of the entry door and in the way. I asked him to move his car and he wouldn't, so I attempted to kick him through the window. He jumped out of the car very fast and was on me like "ugly on an ape". He then smashed my head against the sidewalk a few times and cut it open. That was the end of that one. I lost and some of my friends took me to the hospital for stitches. It was not one of my finer moments. There were many more fights, pretty much weekly.

We often drank in our cars. If we stayed in the apartment, freeloaders would show up. One time I was in the back seat of Pete's car drinking with friends, Pete, Ron, and Ray. We were at the end of a long dirt road near the river. All of a sudden, a car turned onto that dirt road and was slowly approaching us. Ah shit! It was a cop car.

With two of us in the front and two in the back, we quickly devised a plan. We would slide close to each other and try to drive past them like we were two couples of cuddling lovers enjoying the evening. It was very stressful driving out but we went by the cops slowly and luckily they didn't bother to check us out. We hoped that they would think what we wanted them to think, that two couples had parked to neck. It was a really good thing they didn't pull us over. It would have been quite embarrassing for us if they saw that we were all guys because homosexuality was frowned upon back then and not yet legal.

I also worked at an office supply store as a truck driver/swamper (one who assists the driver in deliveries or for relief of driver fatigue). That company sold desks, office furniture, and stationary. I was working there when I met my wife. We used to load desks and office equipment listed on order sheets and deliver them to oil companies. Once in a while, we'd load an extra one to sell privately, mainly to Chinese customers. One time, a police sergeant approached us and wanted to buy a "'hot" desk. We told him someone was leading him astray because we didn't "sell" desks, we "delivered" them. One of our Chinese customers must have told him about us while the sergeant was in their restaurant.

It's a good thing we didn't sell him one, because later when I got on the police department this particular sergeant was one of my supervisors, and I'm sure he would have initiated charges against us. Once on the police department, he didn't recognize me but I remembered him..

Part Five:
Life After Marriage

MY WIFE AND I met when we were both eighteen years old. Back in those days they held an event to raise money to help children in Africa get decent medical care, food, water, and clothing. The event was called "Miles for Millions". Hundreds of individuals participated and signed up sponsors to donate money for each mile they walked. That money was then forwarded to the above charity. It was similar to the modern cancer funding events we now have to raise money for cancer research.

A girl who had been sponsored by our teen hangout had sprained her ankle and wasn't able to do the walk. After a few drinks a few guys came up with an alternate plan.

My wife was that girl, a gorgeous chick, and she agreed to ride in a shopping buggy. Six of us took turns pushing her at running speed around the route. One would push until he was tired, then jump onto an open convertible following along beside her to change places with one of the others.

For me, it was love at first sight. I even jokingly told my buddies I was going to marry that chick. Later, I saw her in our teen nightclub. We bumped into each other while we were both circulating through the crowd trying to bum cigarettes from people.

We had that in common as well. What we didn't have in common was that she was a hippy and I was a greaser. She was all about flowers and "peace", and I was all about fast cars, fights, and "piece". We both had (peace/piece) in common, but they had different connotations.

I didn't think she remembered me, so I introduced myself to her and she invited me to sit down with her and her friend. Sadly, she didn't remember me as one of the guys who had pushed her in the charity walk. Later that evening she said she had to drive her friend home and asked me if I would like to go along for a ride. Of course I would. We had lots of opportunity to talk and became very comfortable with each other. From that day on we'd meet with each other at every opportunity.

I was living in a converted garage that was behind our landlord's house. I had two roommates in that garage. The agreement between us three, was that if we had a girl over, we were to put a bottle in the window. This would let any roommate returning home know that they might be interrupting something and should stay away. I'm sure you get the picture. The landlord's house next door also had a room in the basement that a single male adult was renting. Our garage did not have any bathroom facilities so we were permitted to use the bathroom in that basement. The bathroom was right next door to the basement dwelling tenant's room.

We had several parties in that garage. The amount of rent we were paying was quite high, so we believed there was no threat to us of ever getting kicked out because of noise or too many people hanging around. My wife and I were exclusively dating now and had become intimate, so during one of the parties we had the urge to be alone. However, being alone together in the garage was not possible with so many people in there all the time, so we went next door to use the basement dweller's bed. Of course nothing happened because after lying on the bed for about ten minutes talking, the tenant returned home.

Now this really put us in a panic. If this guy came in and saw us, we had no idea what would happen, but we were pretty sure the shit would hit the fan. I had no idea who the guy was, what he even looked like, or how big he was.

I came up with a plan to knock the guy out when he walked through his door so he didn't know who or what hit him. I picked up one of his shoes off the floor and waited for the door to open. Remember, I was only eighteen years old and did not realize what a stupid plan that was. Sorry to disappoint you though, if you were expecting this story to end in violence or romance, it did neither. The bathroom was right next door to the tenant's room, it was the first room that he visited before going to bed for the night. As he passed by his room and went straight to the bathroom, we had the opportunity to escape without incident. I must have a really good guardian angel because that could have been a mistake that would have followed me for the rest of my life.

We left that room and went back to the garage and enjoyed the party. But within a few minutes, my lady looked at me and said, "Oh my God! I left my purse over there." I'm going to disappoint you again though because she ended up finding her purse and we did not have to go over there to retrieve it. Until then it was really quite concerning. The entire event could have really gone bad, but I was extremely fortunate that I didn't follow through with my plan. Extremely fortunate!

I mentioned that we paid so much rent there that we had no concerns of getting kicked out, but once again I was wrong. We did get a notice to move out because the landlord was not happy with us as tenants. Go figure!

He made it quite uncomfortable for us and was hassling us almost every day. We decided to get out of there before the end of the month rather than wait it out. Because the garage had no bathroom we mostly used empty milk cartons to pee in rather than run next door to use the bathroom there or we just peed outside.

We kept the milk cartons full of pee under the sink. We collectively agreed that because this landlord was so nasty to us, we would dump out about six or eight milk cartons of pee into a pot and leave it on high heat over the stand-alone heater in the garage. (It was small, gas-fired, three-foot-high unit in the corner.) We turned the thermostat for that heater up all the way just before we left. I can imagine that the landlord probably found that quite nauseating, but we felt the revenge was warranted. For some reason he didn't return our deposit.

You might say we moved up in the world because our next place was a big house and had a full bathroom. The downside was that the place was crawling with crab lice, something we found out "itch-identally"! I called my wife-to-be and told her we weren't alone in the house. She got slightly crabby with me.

My wife and I had been dating for about 5 months when she informed me we were going to have a close relative visit us and she hoped it was a boy. I know I was not the fatherly type but I was madly in love with her and wanted to get married. We discussed it in depth and agreed to take the plunge. The mother of one of my friends worked in a jewelry store and co-signed for her wedding and engagement rings. As soon as I got them I created the dorkiest proposal a lady could get. I pretended I had a flat tire in the snow, got out of the car to find the ring in whatever pocket I had it in. I found it and got down on one knee in the snow with the car door open and asked her to marry me. She was in the nice warm car with the heat on. Thank God she agreed before my knee stuck to the frozen ground.

I mentioned I had 2 room mates in the house we were renting. My possessions consisted of a 1955 chev 2 door hard top a couple of pairs of jeans, cowboy boots and some T-shirts, oh, and two pairs of dirty socks. My room mate Larry loaned me a suit and a shirt and I washed my socks the morning of my wedding. It was a big wedding, in a church full of people and when all was quiet, I could hear the sound of my wet socks squishing around in my shoes when walking to the alter. We didn't have much money but we did have a home to go to. We had rented a basement suite but the bed was void of linen. We had my wife's younger brother grab onto a set of sheets and pillow slips we discovered amongst our gifts. He passed them through the basement window of the in-law's house where the reception was held. I broke the box spring of our brand new bed that night while playing superman, flying through the air onto the newly made bed. Juliet was not impressed with her Romeo that night.

Sometimes, old skeletons show up when you least expect them. As previously mentioned, when I was living with Dad, we had two roommates. One of them was Wayne. I guess I made a lifetime impression on Wayne when he lived with Dad and me. However, talk about a small world. Wayne showed up in the city I was now living in and I stopped beside him at a red light one day. I yelled his name and he looked at me. I gave him the bird and relayed a few unpleasantries on the weasel. He probably thought I was stalking him.

My world was just about to get even smaller. I found out that my fiancé's older brother worked at an oil company with Wayne. Her brother was talking to him at work one day and told Wayne that his little sister was about to get married. He mentioned my name and Wayne gave her brother his opinion of me. It wasn't exactly stellar.

As a result, my wife-to-be's older brother took her aside. He asked her if she was sure I was the guy who she wanted to be with, and he told her some of the tales that

Wayne had shared with him. They were probably all true, but as far as I was concerned, I hadn't done too much that I was ashamed of. However I was a heavy drinker, and I fought a lot on the streets. I also drove the crap out of every car I ever had. I still drive cars and motorcycles the same way to this day. It's all about that adrenaline.

It turns out my wife does have a huge influence on me, and she has managed to trim a few of my bad habits. I don't smoke anymore. I don't drink anymore. I don't do drugs, and I don't gamble anymore. WTF happened? At 73 years of age now,I don't think I can fight anymore either, but I probably wouldn't hesitate to give it a try. I used to love it. (Banking on adrenaline of course).

One time, when my wife and I had been married for almost five years, we were visiting her folks at their condominium. Upon leaving, I noticed that my tire was low. There wasn't a service station nearby, so I tried to speed to the nearest one to pump it up so I didn't have to change it. While I was speeding along, a taxi with a passenger in the front seat decided he was going to play policeman and slow me down. He cut me off and tried to trap me behind him and the car to his left.

That made my adrenaline kick in. I weaved around both cars to cut him off, and then slowed him to a complete stop. I got out of the car and went back to his side window and hit him in the side of the head. I didn't notice his passenger get out of the car, but the next thing I knew, I was falling down with the passenger hanging off my back. He pulled me to the ground. I managed to get up quickly, and we briefly tussled until I went psycho and I went after the both of them. They could probably see the "crazy" in my eyes because they ran around their car. I chased them but to no avail.

When I got back around to the driver's side, I reached in and pulled the key out of the ignition. I threw it over the eight-foot chain-link fence that was along the side of the highway, then I got in my car and left. The last thing I saw in my rear-view mirror was one of them climbing the fence to go after the keys.

I didn't hear from anyone about it so it was my lucky day. My wife was furious at me because our four-year-old child was standing on the back seat watching all this through the rear window and narrating the action to her. I think she thought our kid was now scarred for life.

Our son always complained about not having brothers or sisters so after a few years we filled out an application to adopt a boy a year younger than him.

We were told it would be a while before our order was "filled". A month before Christmas, human resources called us to see if we would take in foster children while we were waiting for a child to adopt. They said it would give us a chance to adapt to the changes when adding a child to our family. It was a bunch of hogwash, but we fell for it.

Then they said, "We have an unusual request." They had a family of four kids, ages two, five, six, and seven, who needed a temporary home until just after Christmas. They were siblings and human resources did not want to separate them.

"What about the adoption?" we asked. "That will remain in process," they said.

Jeez, we were ill prepared to add beds, let alone bedrooms to our house. However we thought we could somehow manage it until Christmas was over. Christmas came and went. We managed to get through it, and the kids went back to their mother.

Then they were taken away from their mom again, and she asked human resources if the kids could be placed back in our home because they enjoyed it so much. We got attached to those kids, so we agreed. They are still our kids now over forty-five years later. The adoption request was processed a year later, and we added a sixth child to our flock. He was seven years old when we adopted him and was killed in a car accident when he was thirty-four years old.

Our kids were like a little gang. If someone fought with one he/she fought with them all. We all lived a very happy and exciting life. We had so much fun when the kids were all home. I used to tow them on toboggans behind my 4x4 on unused, snow-covered roads. The objective was for me to whiplash them around corners so they would fly off into the deep snow. They loved it! The deeper I could torpedo a kid into a snow bank, the greater the applause.

Our kids have always had what they needed: bicycles, cars, pool tables, pin ball machines, musical instruments, a swimming pool, hot tubs, dogs, cats, jobs, etc. For summers, we had eight motorcycles, one for each kid and one each for my wife and me.

I remember teaching one of my sons how to ride a motorcycle. However, I neglected to show him how to stop. I took it for granted he knew how, but off he went at full throttle across a field and into a ditch. Luckily, only a lot of laughs occurred but no injuries. One shouldn't laugh when their kids are in distress, but when he hit the ditch he flew about 15 feet, then rolled over a cow pie.

While we're on the subject of motorcycles, I can only grin when I think back about how the kids solved their refueling issues. It never dawned on me that they were stealing gas to keep their fuel tanks at optimum levels. Their solution was to steal it from me when I wasn't home. How did they do it when I had a lock on the tap that opened the flow to the nozzle on my 250 gallon fuel storage tank? The kids appreciated it very much when I put a ladder up for the fuel delivery driver for easy access to the locked filler cap used to fill my tank up. The driver had a key but where did the kids get one? It turns out, they didn't need a key because they put a syphon hose in through the vent pipe and lined up one behind the other with their motorcycles until each of them had a full tank. No wonder the gas mileage on my truck seemed to be so high. It wasn't my truck that was burning all the fuel.

I don't know which one of the little buggers took the lead on that idea but I was quite proud of their ingenuity.

We probably drove the neighbors nuts with all our activity. But sometimes we had the odd issue with a neighbor. In one of the houses we lived in, our neighbor had a dog that was caged except for when his pen was being cleaned. One of our kids came home to tell us the neighbor's dog had just bit him. I thought there had to be a reason so I said, "Just leave the dog alone and you won't get bit."

However, the following week my wife told me that this particular dog was running around again and was in our front yard. I went out to see if I could call it over just to show the kids it was not a danger. Quite a few kids were there when I went outside, and suddenly the dog came to me and bit me in the leg. The neighbor's kid who owned the dog was also there when I slipped up and blurted out, "I'm going to kill that damn thing!"

I like dogs and I'm very good with them, but after it bit me, I knew this one was a problem. Later that same day, my oldest son came racing into our backyard on his bicycle. I was building a fence and saw the dog chasing after him. I picked up one of the two-by-four boards I was using for the fence and clunked the dog on the head, seriously injuring it.

I called the neighbor to explain what had just happened, and he came over to get his dog. I offered to pay his vet bill, but when the vet said it would be hundreds of dollars, and the dog probably wouldn't survive, I revised my offer. I said, "I'll pay for euthanasia, but I won't pay any more considering the circumstances."

There wasn't much he could do. I had already checked with the police who said I had every right to kill the dog because it was on my property, it was aggressive, and a threat to my kids. I did pay the $40, which was, in my opinion, well worth the money to get rid of both that dog and that shitty neighbor.

I was a hunter, but more of a sustenance hunter because we used the meat that was harvested – mostly bear and deer. Deer meat was used in our suppers to substitute beef, but the kids said they wouldn't eat deer meat. We experimented and found that they couldn't tell the difference when we mixed it with spaghetti sauce, and they loved spaghetti. I always loved to watch them chomping away at their deer-sauce-covered spaghetti and always grinned when they went for seconds.

The bear meat was fed to our three Great Dane dogs. If you are ever constipated, you might try some bear meat because it has the effect of creating a volcano in your stomach. The dogs were the ones I learned that from. They shat so much. Then they shat some more. I had to wonder what else was in store. Could there possibly be more on my floor? I failed poetry, got a "P", for poor.

When we had our Great Danes, I made a septic tank out of a dryer drum and threw the dog poop in there over the winter. Come spring it was full. I thought it would filter through the holes in the drum and dissipate into the ground. That was stupid because it didn't. So I put a blue plastic forty-five gallon barrel in the back of my pickup and dumped the dryer drum full of mostly frozen shit into it.

The weather warmed up, it rained a bit, then the shit turned to soup. Damn! I had to get this to the dump and get rid of it. On the way there, some asshole cut me off and I had to slam on the brakes. My wife and I were lucky that I had closed the sliding rear window because when the brakes were applied, 300 pounds of liquid dog shit came towards the cab at a full-speed slide from the back tailgate.

The plastic barrel slammed into the front of the box, and the wet shit flew out of the barrel and painted the entire back window, roof, windshield, and hood. I had to put my wipers on so I could see. It was disgusting, and not much was left in the barrel now. I can just imagine how different things would have been if that back sliding window was open. If it had been open, the kids would have had a much harder time cleaning my truck. Chuckle!

And here's another dump story for you. When we first bought our house in the country, we had a bunch of rocks in the yard. We gathered them all up and had at least a half a truck box full of them. They were a decent size, probably from four up to ten inches in diameter. I told the kids I was going to go to the dump to get rid of the rocks. Three of them came with me – the two girls and the youngest boy. They loved to go there. I had them jump in the back of the truck and told them to hold onto the roll bar.

When we got to the dump I told them to get out of the truck because I was going to open the tailgate, back up really fast from 30 feet away, then slam on the brakes to unload the rocks without any labor involved. I don't like to do any more manual labor than I have to.

They assured me they could hang on because they cleared a place to stand at the front of the box, and they could hold on to the roll bar. At least they thought they could. For the most part they did, except for the little guy because his hands were too small to go around the roll bar. Big sister took care of him though, and she grabbed his arm and hung on saving him from a bruising. I get a big "fail" on parenting for allowing that to happen.

The first bear I ever shot was taken only a block from my house. I saw it hiding in the bushes and drove home quickly to get my shotgun. I loaded it with three slug shells and drove back to where I saw the bear. It was still there, so I stopped, got out of the car, and went down on one knee not more than 25 feet from the bear to take my shot. One shot right between the eyes, and the bear was done. I butchered it in my garage and took the hide to a taxidermist to get a bear rug made. The taxidermist was able to retrieve the slug from the neck of the bear. Being that I shot it between the eyes and the slug was recovered deep in it's neck, he asked me how close I was when I shot it. When I told him "about 25 feet," he said I was lucky to be alive because the bear would have killed me if the shot wasn't instantly fatal.

I had tags for six bears, and my dogs ate most of the meat. Rather than bury the rest I loaded the remaining part of the carcasses into a wheelbarrow. Then in the very early hours of the morning, my wife and I would roll the wheelbarrow into the back of the van to dispose of them. Often, there was blood and guts in the bottom of the wheelbarrow. My wife had to sit in the back and hold it upright until we got to the bush where we dumped them. The downside was that bears smell so bad, and she was gagging all the way to the dumping location while holding onto the wheelbarrow,. Occasionally we had to switch positions because she couldn't stand it anymore.

When I originally bought my bear tags, we went out hunting bears during the day. We took the truck with the kids in the back, and I saw a bear about 40 feet away so I jumped out of the truck and started chasing it. I didn't realize that my kids had also jumped out of the truck and were running right behind me. I shot and hit the bear but only slowed it down and that increased the intensity of the chase, so I went running after it again with all of my kids still in tow. It was irresponsible to have the kids along during a hunt because it could have put them in danger quite easily, but I was young so I'll use that as an excuse.

I kept my garbage in a trailer about 100 feet from my house, and it attracted bears occasionally. I cut a hole in the screen on my deck for the barrel of my rifle to fit through and waited for a bear to show up at the trailer. The kids were all out on the deck with me. It was dark out so I told them that when a bear shows up I wanted them to flip on the spotlights until I fired a shot. Then they were to flip the lights off immediately after the shot. The reason for that was the neighbors would start phoning to see if I was shooting bears again. The answer was: "No. He's at work." Or: "No. He's in bed because he leaves very early to drive to work."

When we lived in that house, it was a moderately populated remote area. That's where I shot most of the bears. One of the old-time residents there owned almost every lot in the development. As he sold them, he charged astronomical fees for putting in septic fields, water lines, and telephone/electrical poles, etc. My mother and father-in-law bought a lot from him and paid more than it was worth. Then he was over there constantly bumming free drinks and trying to get more money for utility services he promised to install at a lower rate. If they agreed to let him do the work, he would always find a reason to add to the end price. I held that against him, and as a result, I never got along with him. He felt the same way about me.

I shot a bear that was at my garbage one night, and the next morning this fellow came over to investigate. It was really none of his business! I had the bear in a wheelbarrow not too far from where we were arguing. Apparently he also called the police before coming over, and he brought a friend of his along for support. My neighbor and my in-laws also came over to support me, so there were about ten or twelve of us standing there yelling at each other when the cop drove up the driveway.

I didn't know he had called the cops, so as soon as I saw the cop car pull into the driveway, I had one of my boys take the wheelbarrow over to the neighbor's house, hoping the cop would not see the bear. I don't know how he missed it because my son was rolling the damn wheelbarrow down the driveway right next to the police car and passed him. I guess his attention was focused on the crowd of people who were yelling at each other instead of a kid pushing a wheelbarrow.

When the cop got out of his car, he just shook his head and said, "Jesus! It's like Deliverance here! What is going on?" I identified myself to the cop as the property owner and told him that these two gentlemen were on my property uninvited and I would like them to get off but they were refusing to leave.

The cop said he didn't know why he had been called out in the first place. Neither did I, but I did request that he tell these two that they had to get off my property so he did. I looked at them and I said, "LEAVE NOW, PLEASE!" They slowly started walking down my driveway and just to taunt them a little bit, I yelled, "RUN!" The cop was shaking his head saying, "Take it easy. Take it easy. They're leaving."

Living in that neighborhood was not unlike the Hatfields and the McCoys, who were at war with one another. In fact there were a lot of similarities. While living there, my neighbors knew I hunted bears, so they would call me when they had a problem bear. People in the neighborhood always referred to "that bear" when they saw one. I'm thinking, "Which one are you talking about?" There were so many bears out there that you rarely saw the same one twice.

It was very dark one night when my next-door neighbor phoned for my help. I must say that it was pretty intense going to my neighbor's yard because a bear was busting up his fruit trees. I didn't use a flashlight because it limits your vision. I could hear the bear, but I couldn't see it. Once I approached, it took off so I continued to follow the snorting sounds it was making while it was moving along the fence line. I stopped when the bear stopped. I couldn't see it, but I could still hear it, and I was pretty sure it stopped in the corner where the fence took a right-angle turn. I took my shot and holy shit I had no idea a bear could scream that loud!

I damn near crapped myself because I thought he was coming at me in attack mode, so I fired again and he stopped screaming. Thank God, because the shotgun only had three rounds and I now only had one left.

I had already maxed out my bear tag limit, and I previously had shot another bear over my limit that was damaging another neighbor's trees and garden. I did call fish and wildlife to report the first one, but now had to tell them about another. I knew the wildlife guy a bit because he had been out to warn me about shooting bears and had told me, "No more!"

This cornered bear was shot about three days after I shot the first one. "Why did you shoot this one?" he asked.

"Because it was breaking off the branches on George's fruit tree, and he called me for help."

The warden said, "Well take it to the dump, bury it, and don't shoot any more bears."

"Okay," I said, "but no promises." I took it to the dump in the morning. I didn't bury it either. I hid it in the bush, and it only took three days for it to completely disappear other than a few clumps of hair. Every part of the bear had either been eaten or was hauled away by other wild life. For the most part nature takes pretty good care of itself.

The old fella next-door taught me how to make moonshine, and he and I had a great relationship. When I shot bears it was often right in my backyard. He called me over one day and said, "You shot a hole in my garage!"

He took me over there and pointed out a square hole, which is not possible with a bullet. I said "George, you need to get new glasses, the hole is square! We both had a laugh and I was off the hook.

The old guy next-door was shooting birds on his own property. When he was looking through the scope while resting the rifle on his car, the scope was of course up high. The scope crosshairs showed a clear target, but the barrel was pointing directly at the fender. He shot a hole in it.

Our kids used to play all over the neighbourhood and they were in a farmers field one time with one of our Great Danes. The guy that owned the land was a grouchy old prick and when he saw the kids out there he went out with a shotgun and ordered them at gun point to go back to his house where he gave them a good scolding.

When the kids came home they told me what happened and I went ballistic! At first I thought they were making this up but because all six kids were involved I was pretty damn sure that it really happened. I jumped in my truck with two of my boys so they could show me the place where this occurred and I banged on the door.

When he answered I was in quite a hostile mood and I said you took my kids into this house at gunpoint! What the fuck is the matter with you! At that point he kicked me in the leg and then ran back into his house. I ran in after him and kicked him in the ass and then left.

If he had called the police on me and wanted to charge me with assault I think I would've had a stronger case against him for both assault and kidnapping. When I got home, the boys were all excited and ran into the house to rat me out to the wife. "Mom, Dad this, and then Dad did that! Blah, blah! Blah! By the time I got into the house, there was no way in hell I could possibly frame the events of that day in any way that could possibly please my wife and she let me know it! Hopefully the crazy bastard learned a lesson. I believe my wife was thinking the same about me.

Our house bordered crown land, which also made us neighbors to the coyote population. We had a couple of cats, and soon I started to see coyotes checking out the kitty buffet in broad daylight. That was unusual, so before they got any braver, I shot one a hundred feet up the hill right behind the house.

The coyote was down for the count. However, my neighbors likely heard the shot so I disappeared for a while until they gave up trying to figure out where it came from. Then an hour or so later, I told my son to go up the hill, but to do so quietly because the neighbors would be able to see him up there. If he was noisy, they would look out to see where the noise was coming from.

I said, "I want you to discreetly push the coyote down the hill until you can no longer see any of the neighbors. Then, I'll take over and get the coyote, throw it in the back of the cube van, and drive it out to the bush to dump it."

I erred in giving him instructions. I forgot to tell him what "discreetly" meant. He went up there, and once he reached the coyote, he started holding his nose and yelling, "IT REALLY STINKS. EEEW! DOES IT EVER STINK." He was simultaneously kicking it down the hill. I should have shot the damn kid!

Anyway, he finally kicked it to where I could get it, and I threw it in the back of the cube van. Then I saw one of our cats. My mind went into "warped mode", so I went over and picked up the cat. The coyote stink on me put the cat in a "get me the hell out of here" mode, and it damn near scratched my chest off. After I got the claws out of my chest, I threw the cat into the back of the truck with the coyote. I don't think its feet even hit the floor. It was running away before it landed in the truck. It flashed by me and ran down the driveway so fast I could hardly tell where it went. I had no idea a cat could run that fast. That was quite an interesting experiment.

I used to catch squirrels in a live trap because they got into things that they shouldn't, such as wiring in our vehicles. My wife insisted I drive somewhere and and release them. My wife, being an ex-hippy, has a tendency to save and protect the world. I was concerned the squirrels would return, just like I would if someone dropped me off a mile or two from home.

To prove my suspicions, I painted the squirrel's tail with red paint and then drove down the road to release the critter. The tail wasn't quite dry when I dumped it out of the trap. How would I know that? The instant that squirrel hit the ground, it ran up my leg, up my chest, and leaped off my neck, leaving a trail of red paint. When I returned home and told my wife what happened, she was unsympathetic and simply said, "Karma, dumb ass," and walked away laughing.

Then I caught a skunk in a live trap. I took it to a creek to let it go. Damn thing wouldn't leave the trap when I lifted the door. Plan "B" then, so I closed the cage door and carried it to the creek and opened the trap door again. The skunk wouldn't leave, so I picked the trap up and swung it as hard as I could to try and rocket it out into the water. It didn't rocket out at all but it dropped at my feet. I ran like hell thinking I was about to get a "Pepé Le Pew" shower.

Six times my dogs got sprayed by skunks, and my wife got sprayed once while thinning rhubarb. Surprise, honey, I hope it didn't get my rhubarb!

Another time, I saw a skunk crawl under my wooden shed. The shed was on skids so I lay down to shoot under the shed using a shotgun. That's not easy to do because the recoil on a shotgun is severe, and you can't pull it against your shoulder to absorb the impact while lying on your side.

I lined up the gun between the skids on the shed. I fired and the shotgun damn near tore my finger off when the recoil on discharge slammed it backwards past my shoulder. I also neglected to pay attention to what was on the other side of the shed; my tractor and a farm truck! Damn! I'm not telling the wife about this one.

So remember how I said my neighbor taught me how to make moonshine? Well, I got pretty good at it. When I made moonshine I used to run it through the still three times to get it up above 90% pure alcohol, because in the condensed form, it took up less storage. The kids figured out that there was no way I would know if they diluted it a little bit. They diluted it, and then they traded moonshine with their friends, who were more than happy to trade it for beer. I guess I taught them well. Perhaps they learned from me through osmosis!

Part Six:
Now I'm a Cop

THINKING BACK, I remember when I was applying for the police department. One of the steps that I had to go through was the interview. It was held at police headquarters in a boardroom with a long table and about eight senior police officers, one probably a deputy chief or somebody else high-ranking, sitting around it.

I was called in from the hallway and directed to sit at the head of one end of the table. I strolled down and halfway there tripped over an extension cord. The only thing going through my head at that time was: Damn, did I ever screw up here, walking into a room full of these guys and tripping. I look like an idiot.

They were pretty good about it, however, and before I left the room, they told me that the interview went well, but I was a little young being only twenty years old. However, they were still going to hire me because I was married and had a son and that gave me some stability. The only other issue was that I was 15 pounds too light because they required individuals to be at least five foot ten inches and 160 pounds. I was only about 145 pounds.

So one more obstacle I had to overcome was to pass the physical. I ate and ate – potatoes, cake, whatever I could get my hands on until I weighed in at 158 pounds and I passed the physical.

When I started on the police department, one of the lecturers told us, "The only difference between you guys and the criminals on the street is that you guys have never been caught and they have." To me that rang true.

I was a cop for four years from 1968-72, and there are so many stories on a job like that. Police recruit school was an experience I'll never forget. We had a sergeant major who was a bit of a narcissistic sadist. In order to show us some self-defense techniques he would call up a volunteer and use him as a crash test dummy. When my turn came, the sergeant major lay down on the mats and said, "Kick me in the stomach."

I hesitated because I didn't want to hurt the old guy, but he lost his patience and said, "Come on, get with the program!" Okay, I thought, it's time to teach this guy a lesson. So I walked over and kicked him in the stomach much faster than he anticipated. He intended to grab my leg and flip me over to impress all the recruits. It didn't happen. My successful assault on him turned out to be a mistake because I then became his lab rat for the rest of the self-defense training.

We were also given instruction on interrogation techniques. A lot of deception is involved in obtaining confessions, but the most valuable information I absorbed was to split up or threaten to split up multiple offenders. If you leave them in separate rooms and ignore them for about fifteen minutes, their minds begin to imagine what might be happening: Are they questioning my accomplice and is he talking?

The funniest interrogation I attended was with a detective who was really good at interviews and had a pair of suspects who had been arrested by other detectives. The two of them were separated for over twenty minutes before he questioned the first one. Then he said to the guy, "There's a guy in one of the other rooms that says he knows you. His name is John Smith, do you know him?"

"Yes, sir."

"Then come with me and point him out." He first opened a door to a room occupied by a plain-clothed cop and said, "Is that him?"

"No, sir.

The detective knew that so took him to the room John Smith was in. He opened the door, pointed at John Smith, and said, "Is that him?"

"Yes, sir."

Then he closed the door and put the guy back where he was originally. Then he went back to John Smith and said, "Well John, you are in a bit of trouble tonight because your friend just fingered you as his accomplice. You just saw him identify you when I pointed at you. You heard him, didn't you? Now, if you'd like to tell me your side of the story, we can close this case off. So what were you two up to tonight?"

John Smith was so pissed off at his friend for ratting him out, he happily volunteered all the facts and signed a confession. Then the detective took that confession back to the first guy and threw it on the table. "Now that your friend has implicated you, I'll need you to write down your side of the story." It was quite impressive to witness. Each one of them only confessed because he thought the other had thrown them under the bus.

That story emphasizes one of the qualities of a good policeman. Now, I'll share a story about how a bad rookie policeman performs.

I was off-duty one Saturday night attending a wedding reception. After quite a few drinks, my wife and I had a bit of a tiff, and she left the reception. She didn't come back so I went to look for her. We were at a private club that was located in an isolated area high up on a hill with no houses around it. The club was surrounded by other hills covered in deep grass similar to a wheat farm setting. My wife took off through the field and ran into a porcupine. She ended up with 33 quills in her ankle.

I could see her in the distance, but I was pretty drunk so didn't think I could walk that far and decided to jump in the car and drive to her. I tried to drive over there but ended up driving off a four-foot embankment and breaking a tie rod. My car now had to be towed, so I walked back to get help.

A buddy helped me out. A tow truck got my car out, and my buddy drove my wife and me to the hospital. Although I was off-duty at the time, my regular shift was on duty when my sergeant pulled us over for speeding.

I told him, "We need a hospital because we have an emergency." He didn't realize I was drunk, but he would soon find out. He said to follow him, and he put on his flashing lights and headed for the hospital. He turned to go to the closest one, but we continued on to a hospital further away. Why? Because we were drunk! The sergeant eventually showed up at the hospital that we attended and was confused as to why we didn't follow him to the closer one. He was about to find out.

While waiting for the doctor to pull those 33 quills out of my wife's ankle, the sergeant approached me. I was sitting in a waiting room full of people. I blurted out in a drunken slurring voice. "Jeez, Sarge. I'm not going to lose my job over this, am I?"

He quickly ushered me to a place less congested and explained to me that I was not impressing the audience, and it was apparent that I had their attention. Then I apologized to him in my drunken demeanor. He couldn't get out of there fast enough and went back to the peaceful setting of his police vehicle. He was probably wishing he hadn't pulled us over in the first place. I was fortunate that he did not put it on my file, so I got away with it.

A lot of excitement happened on the police department. As a brand new rookie, one of the first jobs I had was to walk the beat. The department had about fifteen beats, and fifteen rookies were generally picked to walk them, usually alone.

My old buddy Jack joined the police department in the class following mine. He was assigned to me as rookie walking a beat one night. It was a cold winter day, so we took refuge in the lobby of an apartment building. Jack was playing around with his handcuffs and cuffed himself to a metal stair railing, but he had forgotten his handcuff key. I told him, "I forgot mine too, so I'll go to the nearest call box and call for a car." I left him there for about ten minutes and returned to tell him the sergeant was on the way.

He went into panic mode until I told him I was kidding and unlocked his cuffs with my key. "You prick!" was all the thanks I got. Jack quit the police department a couple of months later because of the irregular shifts and rarely having a weekend off.

Shortly after I joined, I was walking a beat in the downtown area. There was a new building under construction that had 26 floors in place but no walls around the perimeter.

Just for the hell of it, I went up to the top level to look down and see how far 26 floors appeared to be from there. Once at the top I got to thinking, "What if one or even two guys followed me up to see what I was doing and took the opportunity to rid the planet of a stupid cop by tossing me over the side." Yeah, I had a gun, but the element of surprise would have been on their side.

It would've been a crime that would never be solved because whatever happened would have been looked at as either an accident or a suicide. I actually scared myself to the point where I went back down as quickly as possible. When I got to the ground, my stress level slowly returned to normal, leaving me with thoughts about how stupid it was to go up there in the first place.

Another night, I was walking a beat in the east part of town and checking doors in the alley behind commercial establishments when I stumbled upon a person who appeared to be unconscious. The best way to test somebody's consciousness is to put pressure under the collarbone with your thumb. The harder you push, the greater the pain. Nothing seemed to wake this guy, and I knew he was dead. There was a bottle of wood alcohol beside him, and it appeared that he had consumed most of it, which is probably what killed him.

I had to walk a block back to the call box to call in a "sudden death" because back then we didn't have hand radios. The call boxes were telephones in blue metal boxes attached to telephone poles. They were at face height to allow the beat cops to call or receive calls from the dispatcher. Blue strobe lights were on the very top of the call box poles. That way, if the dispatcher needed to call us, he activated the strobe lights and we went directly to the nearest call box to call him back. There were two to four call boxes on every beat and some were blocks apart, but you could see the strobe from almost any road. When we wanted to call dispatch, we had a key to open the box. Then we cranked the handle and talked when dispatch picked up. In this particular case, since I was a rookie, the detectives took over the reporting and investigation procedure for this sudden death. I left and went back on around my beat.

One afternoon while on patrol in a car with a partner, the dispatcher called all cars over the radio saying that one of our officers needed help because he was hit after encountering a shoplifter at a department store.

We started over in that direction and when we got within about a block of the store, we heard gunfire. The first thought that came to my mind was, Oh, that kind of hit. Until then we had been under the impression that the officer was chasing a shoplifter and was hit by a car while crossing the street. However, the sound of the gunfire registered a much different situation.

As we pulled up near to the gunfire, there were several more shots fired. We weren't there soon enough to be in it from the start, but we were there long enough to know that one officer had been shot in the leg and the bullet severed his femoral artery.

The suspect had gone down to the lower floor of a place that sold firearms and ammunition. A young clerk, just eighteen years old, was behind the counter, and the guy asked him if he could see the .30-06 rifle that was hanging on the rack. The eighteen-year-old clerk handed him the rifle. The guy then turned his back to the clerk, reached into his pocket, and pulled out a handful of shells. Then he loaded the rifle and swung around shooting the kid right through the heart.

When I saw the body lying there on the floor, the clerk still had his eyes wide open with a look of shock and disbelief on his face, but he was very dead. One of the detectives pulled down the victim's eyelids knowing he had passed.

After shooting the clerk, the suspect casually put the rifle over his shoulder and walked over to the escalator, rode up to the main floor, and walked out the front door of the store. In a parking area on a vacant lot next to the store, he saw police approaching him and he fired on them.

The policeman who got shot was bleeding severely from his femoral artery. In most situations when you tear an artery like that, you will bleed out within minutes and die. If it were not for his partner applying pressure above the severed artery to stop the bleeding, John would have died. The femur was shattered as well, so he walked with a limp for the rest of his life and was taken off regular duty.

The gunfire stopped because the shooter ran out of ammunition. He was reaching into his pocket to reload when one of the policemen at the scene ran up to him and put his pistol to the guy's head and said, "Drop it right now or I'll blow your fucking head off."

The guy surrendered. Understandably, the policeman who had an opportunity to shoot the subject in the head was later chastised by several officers for not killing him when he had the chance. He said he couldn't, and he actually quit the police department a few months later. The shooter was arrested and locked up. I was the junior man at the scene, so I was given the task of guarding the clerk's body while it was in the morgue.

The detectives thought the shooter's father might try and kidnap the dead body so that there would be no physical evidence to prove that his son had killed someone. To me it didn't seem like that was a situation that was going to happen, but nevertheless I met them at the hospital where the body of the kid was under a sheet. His foot was sticking out from the bottom of the sheet that covered him, the same as the two other bodies beside him. Toe tags were attached for quick identification. It was a pretty creepy sight.

The morgue was quite spooky because it was on a floor that was under construction. The walls at the time were only at the framing stage, and there was only one light on in the room. It was quite disturbing. I had a chair to sit on while there to make sure nobody came in to interfere with any of the bodies. I don't scare that easy, but it was pretty ominous, and when the doors of the elevator suddenly opened, the hair went up on the back of my neck. I immediately put my hand on my gun. Thank God, it was the detectives coming to collect more evidence from the body and to retrieve his personal items, take pictures, etc. I was able to breathe normally again.

The next time I came across a dead body was when I was checking property in a commercial area. I was in a marked car by myself, and while driving by a dry cleaner in the area, I noticed the front door was ajar. There was a body lying down on the sidewalk keeping the door from closing.

I got out of the car and checked the body for blood, wounds, or signs of violence to determine whether he was killed by somebody or had died for some other reason. There was a strong smell of a cleaner coming out of the dry cleaning building, and I thought perhaps he had been in an atmosphere that was lacking in oxygen and tried to get out but didn't make it.

I called the coroner and the detectives, but they chose not to attend as it appeared to be a simple accidental death, so it was up to me to secure the dry cleaner building and deal with the body. This took a bit of time because I had to locate someone who had a key to lock up. I had forgotten to check his pockets for a key before the body was taken to the morgue.

Anyway, after I made sure the building was secure, I went to the morgue to catalogue any valuables that he had on him. His arms were down at his side on the narrow autopsy table. I was on his left, so I put his left arm across his chest to access his pockets on the left side. I had to get a ring off a finger on his right hand, so when I reached over him to pick up the right arm, his left arm flopped down and hit me in the crotch. Jesus Murphy! Holy sheep shit! I really wasn't expecting the body to move and that scared the shit out of me! (Not physically, just an expression.)

One afternoon, I was leaving the police station in my duty car. When I stopped at the first red light, there was a car next to me with a driver who seemed to be passed out behind the wheel. I got out of my car and opened his driver's door and quickly determined that he wasn't sleeping. He was a passed-out drunk. I reached in and turned off the ignition to prevent any possible movement of the vehicle. I don't know how many lights that guy waited for but at least he wasn't driving anymore.

I put the car in "park" and then applied pressure to the nerve under the collar bone. It woke him up right away, and I asked him where he was going. He said he was taking his girlfriend home. Since he was the only one in the car, I asked him where his girlfriend was and he pointed to the backseat. "She's right there." He pointed to a large brown paper bag on the seat.

That was more than enough proof that he was way too drunk to drive, and I had to arrest him for impaired. That was unusual for me because arresting people for impaired wasn't one of my favorite things to do. There is a lot of report writing involved, and it takes a lot of time, not to mention going to court when they plead "not guilty".

My usual way of dealing with impaired drivers was to let them call a tow truck and wait until their car was on the hook of the tow truck. Then the impaired driver had to be in the cab of the tow truck with the driver who would take him home. The drunk's other "choice" was to not do that and be arrested for impaired driving. There were no twenty-four hour suspensions back then.

I was pretty much the same with traffic tickets. The department had a patrol division and a traffic division. In my opinion, the traffic guys were keeners that just liked to pull people over and hand out tickets. That wasn't my bag. When I started on the police department, they gave me a book of ten tickets. When I quit four years later, I gave four of them back unused.

That's an average of one and a half tickets every year. Lack of traffic enforcement was reflected in my personnel assessment every year, but it didn't seem to affect my paycheck, so I could live with that. Besides, I received four commendations for excellent police work in those four years, so to discipline me for a lack of traffic enforcement would have been counter-productive. The tickets I did issue were more for driver stupidity than for violating the Traffic Act. For example, you'd have to be pretty stupid to pass a marked police car in a school zone while driving excessively over the speed limit.

When I was still walking the beat, I was once posted in the worst part of the downtown area where there were three hotel bars and a lot of drunks and fights. I walked alone most of the time. Once, a guy who was quite inebriated stopped in front of me and said, "I think I can take you." He then made it clear that he thought he could kick my ass. I looked at him and said, "I would advise you not to try that."

He laughed and said, "Why not?"

I said, "Because if you try, I'm going to pull out my gun and I'm going shoot you. Now get the fuck out of my way." He seemed to appreciate that tone, and he went on his way.

Once when I was walking a beat that bordered the zoo, I had a new rookie with me to show him the routine. It's rather boring walking the beat, so to make it a little more exciting I showed him how to get into the zoo when it was closed. We just climbed over the fence so all the cages and animals were at our mercy with nobody around other than maybe a security guard. He was normally sleeping in the only lighted building on the premises. Usually the security guards were pretty good with us because most of them wanted to be cops some day.

I showed the new guy where the wolves were located in their enclosure. They had indoor and an outdoor space. The outdoor enclosure had a perimeter of chain-link fence. I rattled my keys while approaching their outside area, and they started barking, growling, and carrying on. Normally they wouldn't bark and growl, but I had been there before with other cops.

Once close to the fence, they reacted as expected and when we put our fist against the outside of the fence with gloves on, they tried to bite us. Then we punched them in the nose, which riled them even more. In time, all we had to do was shake the keys to get their attention.

I took my son and wife there once during the day and started rattling my keys when approaching them. I was about a hundred yards away when the wolves started growling and barking, so I stopped before the crowds figured out the reason they were carrying on. I didn't want people to discover some asshole was shaking his keys to upset the wolves. It was entertainment to pass time, but now it's viewed as animal abuse. That I don't understand. In my view, it was a fucking wolf that wanted to eat me.

The next night, we went into the back of the polar bear cage. There was a walkway back there that was used by zookeepers when feeding the bears. There I saw a four-inch-thick branch lying on the cement. Why it was there I had no idea, but I suppose it might been used by the zookeepers to pull out a feeding bowl. Who knows?

I picked up the branch and poked the bear in the chest. If you've ever heard the expression "don't poke the bear", I can sure as hell tell you why! The polar bear grabbed that branch with one arm so fast and pulled it right out of my arms. I almost came with it up to the bars. Had I fallen into the bars, I can only assume that the bear's next move would have been to grab onto me the same way. That was the closest I came to shitting my pants without actually shitting my pants. (I mentioned shitting my pants here because I actually did that while on that job, but that is another story for later.)

Next we went over to the great ape house to tease the gorillas and large apes. They were not outside, so to get into their enclosure I had to pick the lock on the man door. After I picked the lock, we went inside where there was thick glass between the gorillas and chimps, and another glass between the animals and us.

We banged on the glass to get their attention or get some reaction, but it didn't seem to be much fun. It was getting close to quitting time, so we thought we better head back to the call box to call dispatch so the nightshift officers could go home. We attempted to leave but discovered the way out was also locked and would have to be picked the same as the lock coming in. "Damn!" I never noticed the door had locking knobs on both sides. I tried for ten minutes to pick the lock and couldn't do it. The dispatcher expects to get calls from all beat policemen at or near quitting time, and it was pretty near quitting time.

Until every officer working at night reported in, no one was permitted to leave. At shift end, the guys working nightshift stand in the hallway waiting for the last one to arrive or report. If the last policeman did not report in, everyone had to go back to their cars and go out to find them. We really didn't need that to happen because it would be very bad for us.

Then I heard voices outside the great ape house doors. There was a quarter-inch space between the double doors. One side was locked with a slide lock top and bottom; the other side had the double door-knob locks I was struggling with. I looked through that quarter-inch space and saw a group of zookeepers walking together on their way to work. I yelled out through it to get their attention. One of them approached the doors, and I did my best to communicate with him.

I said, "We are policemen and when checking this building, the door was open so we came in and looked around. When we tried to get out, we noticed that the door self-locked behind us after we entered. We are now locked in here, and we would really appreciate it, if you could get a key and let us out."

"Sure," he said. "I'll be right back." I think he then caught up to his friends and said, "There are a couple of stupid-ass cops locked in the great ape house, and they're waiting for me to let them out, but that's not gonna happen! Ha ha ha ha!" They all probably had a really good laugh.

When nobody showed up to let us out, my partner and I decided the best bet for us would be to kick the door to break it open. We could pay for the damages once we made the call to the dispatcher saying we were okay. Thank God, the doors opened outward or kicking them open would not have been an option. I gave the door a good hard kick and the top and bottom slide bolts split that side of the door so both sides flung open. We then went to the security office and told the security guard that we had gone into the ape house because we found it open, but had to break the door when we couldn't get out any other way. Like I said, security guards were generally pretty good with us, and he said, "Don't worry about it. I'll take care of it."

I said, "May I use your phone to let dispatch know that we're finished our shift and on our way home."

"Sure" he said. "Help yourself."

I phoned in, and we made it through that dilemma. If dispatch had sent the shift out to look for us, they would not have found us easily. If they did, I can't imagine the nicknames they would have had tagged us with for the rest of our career: Monkey Boys, Ape Hangers, Gorilla Guys, etc.

Previously, I mentioned almost shitting my pants. I hate to say it, but in one incident it wasn't "almost". It happened when I was in a patrol car. I went to work with a bad stomach when I should have stayed home. That eventually turned into a bowel problem. That night I was riding shotgun while my partner drove.

I thought I could squeeze out a fart, so I gently relaxed the sphincter to allow some gas out when a surprise spurt ejected from within. I was thinking, Geez, did that really happen?

I had to check just to be sure. I reached down the back of my pants to test the possibility that perhaps it was only a fart. Damn! Now I have two problems: One in my pants, and the other on my hand. I couldn't even open the car door with that hand now. I had to tell my partner I had a situation that needed immediate attention. He was not impressed but did drive me to the nearest service station where I could clean up my act. Nothing like hopping around on the wet floor of a service station in your stocking feet balancing on one foot to get your pants off. My gun fell on the floor. Now it was contaminated as well. What a night! Funny now, but not funny then.

Another time, I was passenger in a patrol car and went by a high school. My window was down and a group of smart-ass high-school boys started to "boo" us when we drove by. My natural instinct was to flip them the bird, so I did! They all started cheering.

That was unexpected, but also unexpected was being called to the duty inspector's office at shift end because someone, perhaps a teacher, thought a cop flipping the bird was inappropriate. I explained the situation to the duty inspector, and he laughed and said, "Please don't flip people off out there. I have better things to do with my time than handle frivolous complaints." I felt it was worth it! Thankfully, our superiors almost always had our backs.

Another night, I was working in an area that was close to police headquarters and went in for our break because it was handy. All of a sudden, someone came running in to the lunchroom and yelled, "Someone just shot the doors out of the front office."

The room emptied instantly as we all ran for our cars to chase the guy. The radios were hopping. We soon learned that an active soldier had pulled into a service station for gas. At that time there were no self-serve stations. The employee there approached the soldier to see how much gas he wanted and then he pumped it. When the employee tried to collect, the soldier asked him if he'd ever been shot. "No," said the employee.

"Well, you have now!" he said and then he shot him. Luckily, the guy did survive the shooting.

Then the solider called headquarters and told the dispatcher that he had just shot a guy and told him where the shooting took place. The dispatcher initiated confrontational dialogue with the soldier after learning the shooting was simply for a thrill. The dispatcher called the soldier a coward and a gutless asshole and said, "If you are not a coward, why don't you come down here and take us on like a real man and prove how brave you are?" The guy came down all right. He shot at the front doors, shattering the glass.

The chase was on! One car managed to locate the guy and box him in so the soldier took cover in a dark wooded area. Gunfire was exchanged until the soldier stopped shooting. One of the policemen involved yelled out to everyone else, "I got him!"

The soldier immediately replied, "Like fuck you did!" but then he wanted to surrender. He was taken into custody and charged accordingly. I believe the military might have taken care of the sentencing because he was turned over to the Military Police. That was standard procedure for dealing with soldiers.

The Military Police were extremely hard on their prisoners back then. I used to stop in there occasionally to bullshit with them. One time they had a guy in there that they figured needed "an attitude adjustment". They actually hosed the poor bugger down while he was in his cell. Not just a fun squirt of water either. They kept the hose on him for several minutes. I couldn't believe how sadistic those fellows were. Army discipline, I guess.

I was working in the northwest part of town. There was a satellite police station there that was unmanned, but it was still used as a lunchroom. One of the guys working in a nearby area managed to catch a porcupine using an old garbage can. He wanted to let it loose in that lunch facility. We all thought this would be a great prank. We couldn't wait around to watch the fun though, because we had just received a call that we had to attend to immediately. It was easy to imagine how surprised the guys would be when they entered to have lunch and there was a porcupine inside. We chuckled all the way to our call.

The call was for a "sudden death" at a house party. We arrived quickly at the residence, and it was packed with kids aged fourteen to eighteen. We entered without knocking because everyone else was coming and going that way. Oddly, no one appeared to show concern about a death in the house. Most at the party were probably unaware until a young girl came running up from the basement.

There was a lot of booze at the party, but we were more concerned about who was reporting a death and how, why, and where it occurred. This girl quickly took us down to the basement where another young girl was hanging by the neck from the wooden one-by-four strapping that was

nailed perpendicular to the joists above us. She had used an electrical extension cord to hang herself by jumping off the bed. I asked the first girl why no one there tried to get her down. She said she didn't know what to do. Considering her age, I had to accept that as
understandable.

My partner and I immediately ran over to the girl who was hanging. I lifted her up to create slack on the knot while he untied it. I put her on the bed and initiated heart compressions in an attempt to revive her even though it appeared it wouldn't be happening. This was the first time I ever tried to give any form of CPR to anybody. Since then, I've done it half a dozen more times.

When the ambulance got there shortly afterwards, they put her on the floor and continued with heart compressions as well as adding rescue breaths. They told me that she should have been placed on the solid floor before my compressions were given. The bed did not give enough support because she was bouncing when my compressions were applied. If she were on the floor in the first place, it would have given support to prevent that. I'm pretty sure that she wouldn't have survived anyway because to me she appeared very dead when we got there. She had already been hanging for several minutes, but I did screw up on my first aid according to what the ambulance guy told me.

We eventually learned that this fourteen-year-old girl had come to the party to try and convince her ex-boyfriend to get back together with her. The boyfriend was with another girl in the living room upstairs. We were told he rejected the subject and that made her so distraught that she went into the basement and hung herself. I didn't bother to question the ex-boyfriend any more because I was quite sure he would have nothing more to add to my report. I was shocked as to how in hell a party could go on with a young girl hanging in the basement.

This incident turned into a real "cluster" after the girl was pronounced dead. I called her dad to give him the painful news about his daughter. He wanted to see her, understandably, and we needed him to identify the body. I presumed she would be taken to the closest hospital so we met him there, but she didn't arrive.

I called dispatch and told him to call the ambulance and find out where she was taken. The dad was quite pissed off by now because we had lost the body, but I could understand why that upset him. They took her to a hospital further east. It's absolutely heart breaking to have a father identify his deceased daughter especially after learning that she died needlessly over a teenage romance. It makes me cry just writing about it.

Another time, I was working with a partner when we received a call that there was a domestic disturbance and a sudden death in a residence in the area adjoining ours. Apparently there was a violent murder there and curiosity enticed us to attend. When we got to the residence, several police cars and the detectives were already on scene.

Apparently two kids in their teens who had been abused by their father decided to end the abuse once and for all. As he walked in the door that night, they hit him in the face with an axe and then kept on whacking at him until he was no longer recognizable. There was blood everywhere from what we could see from the outside looking in. We couldn't go inside due to possible evidence contamination. The kids, now in the back of a police car, were covered in blood as were the doors, walls, furniture, and of course, the axe. The scene was a blood bath and the man was pretty much mutilated and very dead.

I was on day shift in a different area when we got a call first thing in the morning about another sudden death. When we arrived at the house, the caller told us there was a guy in the garage that had left his car running to commit suicide. When we went back there, the car was no longer running because it had run out of gas.

So besides doing another sudden death report we called the coroner. He was not available so we called an ambulance to transport the body. When they arrived they wanted help getting the body out of the car. He was lying down in the back across the whole seat. Since he had been there for quite some time, rigor mortis had already set in, so he was pretty stiff. At least he would be easier to lift because he wouldn't bend easily.

In that state, the blood flows to the lowest point of the skin on the underside of the body and that skin turns purple. I knew all that. What I didn't know was that when I grabbed him by the ankles to pull him out, he had been dead long enough that his ankle skin peeled off in my hands. "Ah fuck! That's disgusting!" I realized I should have had gloves on.

You'd think that would be the worst thing that happened that day, but it wasn't. When I got him partially out of the car, the ambulance guys took hold of his legs. I then moved up the body to lift him from under his lower back and buttocks to lighten their load while my partner waited to lift his upper body. As soon as we lifted him, he shit himself and jeez, did it stink! I almost threw up. The bowels often let loose when you move a dead body. Anyway, we got him into the ambulance without me puking.

While on duty in a car working alone, I drove by a service station that was closed. I noticed a fellow down on his knees with a syphon hose inserted in a car that was parked there, and he was syphoning gas into his gas can.

I parked my car around the corner and walked back there as quietly as I could and when I got within three feet of the fellow, I startled him when I said, "What do you think you're doing?"

He turned around and jumped up, dropped everything, and ran. I chased him for about a half a block until he was just about ready to enter an apartment building. I thought if he went in there my chances of catching him would be slim at best, so I yelled out, "Stop or I'll shoot you. I have my gun out!"

Of course I didn't have my gun out, and I had no intention of shooting him, but I thought if I used that bluff it might work. It worked on TV. In fact, it did work because he stopped in his tracks and put his hands up. He must have watched the same TV show.

Sometimes, I worked with a partner. For a while, I was passenger with a partner whose name was Norm. Norm had a photographic memory. Back in those days, there were no computers – only a sheet of license plate numbers of vehicles that had been stolen. Norm's memory was such that he could remember almost every license plate on that sheet. We were driving down a busy street and the car in front of us was bearing one of the numbers, so we knew it was stolen.

The guy must have noticed the cop car behind him because he made an immediate left turn. Norm also made the turn to follow him. Norm was a senior police officer with several years on the job, and therefore had a lot more experience than I did. So as soon as the guy turned, Norm said to me, "Get ready to chase him because he's going to stop and he's going to run."

He was right because the guy did stop, and Norm pulled up beside the car on the passenger side to get a quick look at the fellow. Just like he said, the guy opened the driver's door and bolted. I immediately jumped out of the car and gave chase until I noticed that before the guy got out of the car, he had left it in reverse and it was starting to roll back.

I was concerned that if I let the car go, it would back into the busy street that we just turned off and possibly injure someone so, I had to make a decision. Do I stop the car or do I chase the guy?

I decided to stop the car, and because the driver's door was left open, I managed to jump inside and was able to stop it before it backed on to the busy highway. That decision didn't come without incident. My left leg got caught under the door when getting into the car while it was rolling back.

Dammit! I should have chased the bastard! I didn't break anything, but I did sustain a badly bruised shin. Other cars were called in to see if we could locate the suspect, but after a half an hour of circulating around the area, we all had to give up looking for him and he got away.

One afternoon shift, I was part of a drug raid at a house in the northeast part of town. There were about six uniformed members and a couple of detectives involved. The place was a known drug hang out, and the detectives had gotten a tip that on this evening there was going to be a large quantity of marijuana and stolen merchandise there. We had a warrant to enter without permission so the information was stellar.

I was instructed to search for stolen property such as jewelry, clothing, musical instruments, radios, TVs, etc. If I found drugs during my search, I was to inform one of the detectives so that he could tag and bag it to retain continuity in case a court appearance resulted.

I noticed a young girl about sixteen years old who was trying to hide a leopard coat under the bed. I intercepted her attempt and recovered the coat. It still had sales tags on it from a large department store and was priced at over $300, which was a lot of money at that time.

I arrested her for possession of stolen property and secured the coat. Her age was a concern because she couldn't be convicted as an adult, so I placed her in a temporary lock-up until child services could attend. In the meantime, I called her dad and explained to him that she was being processed as a juvenile and was being charged with possession of stolen property.

He was so concerned, he said, "I'll get there as fast as I can to see what I can do about bringing her home, but it'll take me a while. I live twelve hours away from you, and I'll be driving there."

I went home for the evening, and when I got back on shift the next afternoon, he was waiting for me in the lobby of the front office. I was extremely impressed that he had so much concern for his daughter. I dropped all charges against the young lady and released her so she could accompany her dad back home. The coat was returned to the store it was taken from.

Now, for a different kind of parenting story: I stopped a juvenile while he was riding his motorcycle in an unsafe manner only to discover that he had had way too much to drink. Even without using a breathalyzer, it was quite easy to determine that he was operating a motor vehicle while impaired by alcohol.

His motorcycle did not have any lights, and it was after dark. I asked him where he lived to determine whether or not I needed to call the tow truck to come and get his motorcycle. He said he only lived a block and a half from where I stopped him, so I came up with a plan. I made him push his motorcycle the rest of the way home, and when he got there, I went to the door with him to speak with his father.

I explained to the man that his son was driving under the influence of alcohol and said that rather than arresting him, "I thought it would be best to bring him home so that you can deal with him as opposed to me charging him under the criminal code for being impaired while operating a motor vehicle."

The father immediately became curt with me and a little bit belligerent. I thought because I was doing his son a favor, the father should be a lot more appreciative, but he wasn't. So I said to the boy, "Come with me, son, because now you are under arrest for impaired driving." I started walking away with the boy, and I told the father that if he interfered with my arrest, I would charge him with obstruction.

The man's attitude immediately reversed, and he became pleasant and much easier to deal with. I gave him a bit of a tongue lashing, explaining that his attitude was not appreciated, especially since I had brought his son back to give him a break. I told him, "I'd like to suggest to you that you give him some sort of punishment. Perhaps explain to him how serious drinking and driving is and what the possible consequences might have been had you not been cooperative. Furthermore, I must say that your son was polite throughout the whole incident, and I commend you for that. He seems like a nice kid." Nothing in this paragraph is consistent with my own behavior. (Don't cry; apply!)

Back then, there were pubs in the city that actually had rooms in the basement or a back office where on-duty cops could sit and drink as long as they wanted. Free! The server brought in glasses of beer as fast as we could drink them, just as if we were customers that tipped well. We were merely cops who took advantage of the vulnerability of establishments that served food and alcohol. Those places liked us to visit because if they had problems with patrons, we were already there or we made it a priority to get there fast.

Many restaurants and bars participated in these arrangements so we rarely paid for meals. If a restaurant charged you for the food, drink, or service, you simply took your time getting there when they had unruly patrons. The fast food places were also on board in offering benefits.

We went into a fast food take-out joint one time and asked the owner or employee if he had seen any suspicious persons skulking around. "Why?" he asked.

"Well, we heard that there was going to be a robbery tonight either here or at the fried chicken joint down the street. This place is a little more isolated, so we're thinking we will park out of sight and keep an eye on you and your restaurant. Could you make us up a couple of orders of onion rings, please?"

He complied while I waited. Then I said, "How much do I owe you?"

"No charge," he said as he thanked me. We left with our free food, but as there was no threat, there was no need to watch the place. Fortunately, he didn't know that.

While I was on day shift one time, we got a tip that a bank robbery was expected to take place in one of the three banks in my area. I was supposed to do frequent drive-bys at those banks. I thought if the tip was valid, there would already be stakeouts positioned at each bank, so I called the dispatcher, who was a friend. I told him I would be at an armored car company applying for a job and gave him a number to reach me if anything happened in my area.

I was looking for a place to work that paid about the same but didn't require me to work mostly night and afternoon shifts. I also had my application in with the fire department. There were no cell phones or portable radios back then for dispatch to reach me. I was only in the armored car company office for about twenty minutes when dispatch called to tell me that one of my banks had just been robbed and to get the hell back there. I went "code 3" with light and siren toward the bank involved.

The info received was that a masked man had robbed it and escaped in a cab (with cab number whatever). I drove around the neighborhood along with several other police cars looking for the cab, and lucky me, I found it parked and still running. Looking around, I saw no one suspicious, so why was the cab running? I shut it off and grabbed the keys to unlock the trunk thinking the cabbie might be in there dead.

The cab driver was in there all right, but he was very much alive and very glad to see me. He said the bank robber told him he'd kill him if he made any noise. As long as the cab was running, he was to supposed to keep quiet.

All in all, finding him made me look pretty good. My area, my bank, and I found the getaway vehicle. Bad guy got away, but three out of four wasn't a bad score.

Once when working New Year's Eve, I got together with five other on-duty cop buddies in four police cars. We decided to collectively round up some liquor from our various homes and meet up in the hills to party a bit. So we did, and we had all four cars up there. Everyone got into my unit to B.S. and drink. We were knocking the drinks back pretty hard, and the bullshit was good, but it wasn't long before things got out of hand.

One of the guys had to piss, so he thought it would be funny to jump up on the hood of my police car and piss on the windshield. The rest of us were trapped inside trying to avoid getting pissed on. While he was pissing on the windshield, I put my wipers on. We were all laughing because we rolled up the windows just in the nick of time to keep from getting splashed.

My car was an unmarked car, and my red flashing light was a small portable. There was another unmarked car there, as well as two police cruisers with full lights and markings. The guy closest to my passenger window opened his window and threw my red light out, telling me it was useless. The cord attached to it prevented it from hitting the ground, but it bounced off the passenger door. Now the crux of this story…

None of us noticed that a car with a couple of lovers in it was parked with lights out just a few hundred feet from us. The occupants likely just witnessed six policemen in uniform being drunk and disorderly in official police vehicles, including one standing on a car and pissing on a windshield, and then someone throwing a light out the window.

Now that we were all aware we had been busted, what could we do? Nothing! We left as soon as everyone got into their respective vehicles, and we just drove off unconcerned about consequences. After all, who would ever believe a couple of young people who might be "cop haters" making such an outrageous accusation? Furthermore, who would have the courage to report it? It's a really good thing there were no iPhones back in those days.

I should also mention that these pop-up police parties happened quite often. Usually if the night was quiet, we would team up and raid an outdoor teen party in one of several locations where we knew they usually partied and had liquor. We'd drive in with flashing lights, using the loudspeaker to announce the party was over. We knew they would scatter and hide their booze before being asked to leave the area, especially if we allowed them to go without being charged for illegal possession of liquor. Then half a dozen of us went hunting for the hidden booze, not unlike little kids at Easter looking for Easter eggs.

One time, my partner and I drove into a nightspot where couples usually parked while necking, and we caught a couple drinking beer. Only a few bottles were inside the car, so we had the guy open the trunk. Whoa there! What do we have here? A laundry tub filled with ice and a couple dozen ice-cold beer lay before my eyes. Bonus!

"Hey," we said, "We aren't bad cops. We should be charging you as minors with illegal possession of alcohol, but we're not going to. If you drive over to the closest garbage can a few hundred yards away and put your beer in there, we will let you off this time."

We pretended to take his word that he would do what he was told to do. Just in case he didn't, we parked out of sight, closer to the garbage but well hidden in the bushes. He did what he was told to do, and we retrieved the cold beer when he left. Then we parked at a nearby location and drank our free cold beer.

One time we were parked and drinking beer when a couple pulled in about fifty feet away from us. What the hell! That's gutsy! I got out of my car and told them they would have to leave the area because we were on a stakeout. I also told them we were expecting something big to go down, so for their own safety they needed to move along now! Of course, that was a bunch of bullshit! After they left, we tried to finish our beer. What we couldn't finish, we'd hide for another time.

While working with partners, I attended several house parties in police uniform, mostly just to party, not to investigate. Yes, those were the days. I just had coffee a while ago with an old friend from almost fifty years back, and we were reminiscing about how my partner and I would crash his parties while on duty.

Please keep in mind that our behavior for the most part on most days was very professional, and I say that sarcastically. For instance, my partner and I got a call to the

5th floor of an apartment to take information for a theft report because a tape deck was stolen from a lady's car. We got on the elevator, but I had such bad gas that I farted. It was a nasty one too. We had only gone up one floor when the elevator door opened and an elderly lady got in. I didn't want her to think I was the one who dropped the rose, so when she glared at me, I put on a look of disgust and looked at my partner. It worked because she then glared at him with the same look of disgust. She got off at next floor. It was so damn funny that I got the giggles just thinking about the position I put my partner in. When we got to the complainant's door to take the theft report, I still couldn't stop laughing even as she opened the door to let us in.

She looked at me and said, "Why do you think it's so funny that someone stole my tape deck from my car?"

I said, "I'm so sorry ma'am, but a lady on the elevator on the way up told us about something that happened to her that was hilarious. My apologies." I stopped laughing until we were on our way down again in the elevator. See how professional we were?

One afternoon shift, my partner and I visited a horse trailer manufacturing business on the outskirts of the city that was friendly toward cops. We used to do a lot of drinking there with the owner. We got into the booze pretty good, and we partied quite heavily. My partner asked me where my uniform hat was, and I immediately clued in that he had done something to it.

I wasn't wrong. He had cut my hat in half on the power band saw. That was pretty funny, but the owner decided to top that stunt. He asked my partner if he could see his revolver. My trusting partner handed it to him at which time the owner shot out a few fluorescent lights, exploding the long bulbs above us. It was his place, so why not help? It looked like fun, so I shot out a couple more, and soon afterward, everyone had a turn until there was only one overhead light still working.

You know how the owner topped that? He cut the barrel off my partner's .38 Webley revolver with the power band saw. What's crazy about that is we were all laughing hysterically. Then just before we left, my partner placed (what was left of) his revolver back in his holster. It flopped over and was now obviously too small for the holster.

"Gimme the fucking thing!" said the owner. Then he welded a two-foot-long piece of pipe to the revolver to replace the missing barrel. When attempting to place it back into the holster, the base of the holster had to be cut out for the pipe to go through it.

Before we reported back to the station to end our shift, we went for a coffee at one of the hotels with the pipe dangling down my partner's leg. No one in the coffee shop seemed to notice. However, maybe we were so drunk that we just didn't notice if there was anyone in the coffee shop.

Before returning to the station we dropped off the hat and modified gun in our personal vehicles. We reported them stolen from our vehicles the next day. Neither of us was disciplined. All's well that ends well!

For night shift, I always carried an alarm clock and an inflatable pillow in my briefcase. One night, my partner and I parked behind a garage in an alley behind some guy's house. The garage was on one side of where we parked and a field was on the other, so no one could see us from their homes. I was stretched out in the back seat, and my partner was in the front. We were awoken earlier than we expected by a knocking on the driver's side window.

It was the guy who owned the house. We were parked behind his garage and blocking him from getting his car out. He needed to go to work. He was so darned polite and quite nervous. "Excuse me, sir, ah, um, sorry to bother you, but you are parked behind my garage, and I need to get my car out to go to work."

My partner apologized and moved the car. I think it was possible the guy never even saw me in the back because it was winter, and the windows in the car were fogged up. We created an excuse in case it was reported. We'd say that I was out of the car on foot, and he was crouching down so he couldn't be seen by some fictitious guy that we were allegedly watching. We'd say the guy disappeared, and we were trying to locate him. Yah, that would work. Luckily the guy didn't complain.

Another time, a lady was concerned that a Peeping Tom was often sneaking up and looking in her windows. We had been dispatched to that location a few times before but were never able to apprehend the culprit. The solution was to place a plain-clothed officer in her garage so that when the suspect showed up, we would use the element of surprise with a "Johnny on the spot" cop in the garage. That was the plan anyway, but it had a couple of flaws. The officer was in the garage at inconsistent times on fluctuating days, and neither the home owner or the police cars patrolling the area would know when he was there.

We were instructed to attend as normal if she did call when the peeper showed up. Well, she called all right, and two cars came from the front – me and another car from the alley. All approached silently because the peeper was in her back yard then. All hell broke loose when we simultaneously showed up in the back yard and faced the man she had seen, and he was armed. We all drew our weapons and the yelling started, "DROP YOUR GUN. DROP IT NOW!"

He did, but he was yelling back at us. No one could hear what he was saying because everyone was yelling. You might have guessed that he was the undercover cop who was in the garage. He went into her back yard to pee and that's when the homeowner saw him.

Fortunately no one was gun happy. It ended well but the peeper would not be apprehended that nigh but perhaps might be when another shift was on duty. It was a good laugh for all of us, but it could have ended in so many different ways.

I was involved in another gunfight one evening. While on shift in a middle-class part of town, I got a call to assist a car that was attending a "shots fired" situation. I radioed the car that got the call and told them I would cover the back alley while they approached from the front. I did drive by the place first because the car that got the call hadn't arrived yet. Then, I drove around to the alley after identifying the place from the front.

While I was getting into position, two traffic cops apparently showed up at the front of the house, also to assist the car that got the call. Instead of assisting, they jumped out of their respective cars and ran towards the house, apparently intending to take the lead on the call. Not protocol, but who ever follows procedure anyway?

The car that got the call arrived seconds later just as a guy came running out of the house. He saw the first traffic cop coming toward him and fired the shotgun he was carrying. The cop went down, and the car that got the call along with the second traffic cop now became engaged in a firefight with the shooter while the downed cop was lying on the sidewalk.

I was in position in the back alley when the shots broke out, so I took cover on the opposite side of my car. I had the radio mike in one hand and my revolver in the other waiting to blast the offender should he come running to the rear of the house towards me. The bullets being fired by the cars out front were zinging past me, breaking off branches on the trees above. Luckily none hit my car or me. If the shooter came out back, I was ready for him, but I sure as hell wasn't going to stand up and get hit by a stray bullet. Nor would I fire a shot when I couldn't see the target.

During this firefight, I visualized myself looking over my pay stub thinking: What the fuck am I doing on this job? The numbers on the pay stub are not near high enough to put up with all this bullshit!

Finally, a few minutes later, a call came over the radio saying the shooter was down. He gave himself up once he had emptied the rounds in his shotgun. Inside, his mother was dead in bed, and his brother lay dead on the living-room chesterfield. The guy had a fight with his brother so he shot him. When his mother heard the shot, she yelled at him from the bedroom. Then he went in to her room and shot her. They were both shot in the face.

The cop lying on the ground was taken away in an ambulance, and it was later reported he had lost an eye and took some pellets from a shotgun round to the groin. The shotgun only held five rounds, so it is assumed the shooter probably reloaded after shooting the two inside. The limited capacity of the shotgun likely prevented the situation from turning out a lot worse.

Afterwards, several of us went door to door to the homes behind me to check and see if any houses had been hit by bullets. I don't know how many shots were fired, but I'd guess at more than a dozen.

Occasionally, I walked a beat in the southwest area of town. When I did a nightshift there, I had an agreement with the clerk at a hotel to wake me up every hour so I could call in after my one-hour sleep stints in the lobby. On one occasion when I left the hotel to make my call, someone must have been watching me go by. He probably thought I wouldn't be back for a while and would continue around my beat, giving him ample time to break into a local dry cleaner. Instead, I made my call at the call box and immediately turned to go back to the hotel to sleep some more.

When I had gone past an empty lot by the call box just minutes before, there wasn't anything on the ground at the rear of a dry-cleaning business. Upon returning, I noticed a plastic bag on the ground. There was a waist-high fence between that bag and me. The police uniform for walking a beat in the winter included what they called a "greatcoat", which was a heavy felt coat that went down to the knees. That coat prevented me from immediately getting a closer look because getting over the fence in it would have been a challenge. Instead, I backtracked to the last driveway. In doing that a building momentarily blocked my vision of the field. It was apparent someone was hiding behind some shrubs and had dropped the plastic bag when he first saw me.

While I was backtracking he must have jumped the fence to avoid me but left some dry cleaning behind. I called dispatch after returning to the call box to get some assistance and patrol cars were dispatched to the area but the guy got away. The detectives wanted to know why I didn't jump the fence instead of going around the building. I said, "Do you think you could jump that fence with this damn coat on?"

Who in hell ever thought that draping a beat cop with ten extra pounds of felt hanging down to his knees might be a good idea? I couldn't even sleep in it because indoors it was way too damn hot.

That was a "bad guy got away story", but it emphasizes how ridiculous some of our uniform clothing was at that time. They had a tendency to copy the British uniforms like the "Bobbies" used to wear. Even if I had seen the guy run away, there was no way in hell I could have caught him when weighed down with that damned coat.

In that city of just over 400,000 people, every day was interesting; not necessarily productive but interesting. One evening my partner and I were quite bored, so we thought we would park and have a sleep in one of the local cemeteries. We found a nice spot to park, but I looked over and about twenty yards away there was a coffin right beside an open hole.

"What the hell? Did someone just dig that up or what?" More than likely it was there in preparation for a service in the morning. But curiosity got the best of us, so we got out of the car and went over to investigate. It looked like an expensive coffin made entirely of copper or at least completely clad with a decorated copper finish. Of course, our curiosity led us to check it out further to see if there was a body inside, and if so, what it looked like. We tried everything to get the coffin open, but it seemed to be permanently sealed.

We assumed that it was sealed for a reason, possibly because it contained a contaminated or diseased body or something along those lines. So we left it and went back to the car and got a few hours of sleep before going off duty. I can't imagine how things would have turned out if there was a body inside. It might have been something that haunted us for life. Pun intended.

Cemeteries were generally a pretty good place to park to pass a few hours away sleeping. One night at a different cemetery, we drove in looking for a nice private place to park and came across a sergeant sleeping in his car. We drove up beside him and tooted the horn, which startled him. He looked over at us and opened his window to give us a feeble excuse for why he was sleeping in his car.

Of course, we kept this to ourselves knowing that sometime in the future the sergeant could come across us while we were having a sleep and we could remind him that we learned by example. I don't believe there was ever any animosity between the sergeants and the regular duty cops because everybody understood that we were "brothers in blue" and we always had each other's backs.

I sometimes think back to the most harrowing chase I have ever been involved in. There weren't very many of them, but this one had me thinking I was going to die – probably because I wasn't driving, my partner was. It started on a busy downtown street and ended about fifteen miles south on a busy highway. We went through at least ten red lights at a high rate of speed. It was absolutely terrifying at each intersection. I kept thinking about the consequences of doing that. On the positive side, the guy we were chasing flew through first so if we were really lucky, he would soon crash.

He did crash, but being that we made it through the miles we covered before that happened was nothing short of miraculous. Finally, he went through an intersection on a busy highway and got T-boned by a car that had the right of way. I jumped out of the car and hauled him out of his car and beat on him for almost killing us all. I wanted to kill him. Then I threw him in the back seat of our car, and he was yapping off so much I told him to shut the fuck up!

He wouldn't, so I backhanded him across the face. He said he was going to charge me with assault, so I hit him again and said to my partner, "Did you hear that? This asshole wants to charge me with assault. Did you see me hit him?"

"No, I didn't see you hit him." Then he turned and looked at the guy and said, "Shut the fuck up before I'm tempted to hit you too." The guy finally shut up. He was taken in and processed for dangerous driving.

More often than not, cops will socialize with other cops. I noticed right away that once I was officially a cop, my friends were backing off quite a bit. Soon you find that you start feeling a friend 'void'.

One time I was invited to go with a group from work to the home of another constable who was more senior than I was for a wine-tasting session while on duty. I went and our host brought us all small samples of different types of homemade wine.

I have never been much of a wine connoisseur. In fact, I have never really cared for wine at all. I only accepted the invitation because I was flattered to be included in this group of senior police officers. However, I'm the type of person who says what's on my mind, and I gave my opinion of each and every sample of wine. You know: one was sweet, one was tart, one was smooth, and then I mistakenly said, "This one tastes like lighter fluid!"

Apparently the host did not appreciate that comment so the next glass that he gave me to taste actually was lighter fluid. I came pretty close to vomiting, but I managed to restrain myself. I did suffer the consequences of that horrible taste remaining in my mouth for the rest of the evening. Next time someone invites me to taste homemade wine, I'll tell them they can kiss my ass, regardless of who they might be.

While working an afternoon shift, my partner and I got a call to a domestic dispute in the northeast. The wife met us at the door and let us in. Upon entering the house, I saw a guy sitting on the chesterfield in the living room and caught a glimpse of him sticking something down inside the chesterfield between the cushions. I told him to stand up and come over to the other side of the room.

He did, and I went over to pull the cushion up. I found a .32 caliber automatic pistol that was loaded and ready to fire. Things could've turned out a whole lot different that day, but it was another one of those lucky days. Why in hell would a guy need to have a pistol in his chesterfield?

It made me wonder if he was after someone in that house. At least I had given them a heads-up that he had it. Guns were not prohibited back then, so I returned his pistol to him when we left. Afterward, I thought, "Geez, I hope he doesn't shoot his wife with it." The dispute had been between the two of them. We weren't called back so I guess they worked everything out.

The next night we were called to another sudden death. It was in the basement suite of a house. Upon entering, we found a body lying in the middle of the living room floor beside a shotgun. There wasn't too much remaining of the left side of his face and there was plenty of skin, shrapnel, and blood all over the floor, wall, and ceiling.

Not much more to investigate there. It was obviously a nasty shotgun suicide, so we didn't bother to call the detectives.

Instead of enduring the unpleasantries of going through his pockets, we decided to let the ambulance guys do it. We just took out his wallet to identify him for the report and to track down relatives. The ambulance guys were obliging, so they helped us retrieve any valuables and we helped them take the body out – after it was on the gurney. I didn't want to go through another poop episode.

While on City Police, I got pulled over for impaired driving one evening and the fellow constable who pulled me over said, "Well you've definitely had too much to drink, so you better head straight home and go to bed." He was a brother in uniform and I appreciated the break. Probably a good thing he didn't see my wife passed out on the front seat. That was because I got out of the car to meet him.

Here is another example of cops protecting cops.

Tom, one of my classmates in the police recruit class, was a close friend. He was some crazy, believe me. He got all liquored up and somehow thought it would be a good idea to drive his convertible with the top down while standing on the floor in the back seat. He had a passenger in the front seat operating the gas and brake pedals. It sounds ridiculous, but it actually did happen. He learned it wasn't such a good idea when approaching a T intersection with the intention of making a ninety-degree left turn. Tom was still in police uniform pants with a stripe on the outside of each leg.

The guy operating the gas and brake had his foot slip off the brake onto the gas pedal. Tom tried to steer through the turn but was now going too fast and ended up rolling the car onto its side, throwing them both out.

Police, fire, and ambulance all attended while spectators gathered. Because Tom was wearing the easily identifiable police pants, curious members of the public watched for news releases. None appeared because a cover-up was initiated by senior police officers. Someone wrote a letter to the editor expressing concerns of a cover-up but to no avail. That's how well our superiors looked after us.

Another story about Tom that happened just before we both became policemen. I was driving my car on a highway at highway speed when a car bumped me from behind. Guess who? Yes, this is how Tom was. He wanted me to come and look at a car we could buy cheap together and sell high.

He had the address of the owner, so we went to see it the night before we intended to buy it. He had brought a quart of oil and under the cover of darkness, he used a funnel to pour the oil into the gas tank of that car without the owner's knowledge. Then in the morning we took it for a test ride and because the oil was mixed in with the gas, the car blew a lot of smoke out of the tail pipe. This made it easy to buy it at a reduced price (much lower than what the owner was asking).

I agree that this was totally unscrupulous but it wasn't my idea. I did think it was an interesting idea though, so guilty there. Tom was quite a bit more brazen than I was, but I certainly wasn't a saint either. All knowledge has value really.

Back to work in my term as a rookie. I was walking the beat one night adjacent to a beat across the street, so after greeting the fellow policeman there, we came up with an interesting plan. We'd team up at an intersection that was controlled by a traffic light. At most traffic-light-controlled intersections there was a box that allowed manual operation of the lights in the event of a failure or to test the bulbs. We had keys to those boxes; it was the same key that opened the metal call boxes.

If you flipped a switch to change the light to yellow and then a split second later the red switch, an unsuspecting driver would go through the red light. The one who wasn't operating the light was standing a little ways down the block to pull the guy over for running a red.

No, we didn't issue tickets. It was just a good reason to pull them over and get a look in the cars without having a reason. Once in a while, we'd get lucky and find stolen goods in cars we stopped. It was also fun.

Occasionally, some drivers that we tried to pull over wouldn't stop. Why? Because a cop on foot can't chase anyone. While that is true, I have to say that many a beat cop went through a flashlight or two after throwing them at the windshield of a car that wasn't prepared to stop. I lost one myself that way.

Another police duty that I was assigned to on occasion was "Paddy Wagon Patrol". In 1968, the City Police paddy wagon was an old 1948 panel truck. When assigned to this truck you were always with a partner. Our job was to drive around city center and arrest obviously drunk people who were walking around or those who were passed out on the sidewalk. We always managed to fill the back of the truck with drunks and bring them to the city cells to book them into one of two drunk tanks. The drunk tanks were large cells about 20 x 20 feet, and most weekend nights there were more than ten or fifteen drunks passed out in each one. Many had pissed their pants.

We had to empty their pockets when booking them. No gloves were used back then, and my hands went into empty their pockets including the pockets of those who pissed themselves. No one ever wore gloves during searches because it was never considered a hazard. Their belts were also taken away to prevent suicide attempts. In the morning all the drunks were released and many of the same drunks were gathered up the next night by the paddy wagon patrol.

When we collected them on that patrol they sometimes got quite obnoxious. I'm not going to say they didn't have good reason to be that way. We used to take corners sharply, slam on the brakes unexpectedly, and pretty much give them a ride from hell. They often barfed in the truck, and the smell back there was quite vile. Those kinds of things don't happen these days because there are so many human rights that now prevent the misconduct of any professional, but it was a lot of fun and no one ever complained.

One of the reasons could have been that none of them could remember the events of the night because they were too intoxicated to recall it. I once asked one of them why he drank toxic drugstore mixtures that contained alcohol. He told me that when you have no money to buy liquor store alcohol, you get the DTs (the shakes when an addiction is not satisfied). The drug store mixtures with alcohol can easily be obtained, and they reduce the DTs. Some drink too much of those poisonous mixtures and die, as you read earlier. Think back to the cars made in 1968.

This is 'the' 1948 truck I drove and gathered drunks with. The fellow in the picture is not me.

Another time we were driving our patrol car out of our assigned territory. We were just cruising, but being as it wasn't our area, it was not protocol. A sergeant spotted our car from a road at a higher elevation, and he radioed, "This is Sgt. Snooper (made up that name) calling the car driving on 82 Ave. Please identify yourself."

"Wow!" He's asking us to identify ourselves, which means he doesn't know who we are and obviously he can't see our car number or he would have called it. Being as we weren't where we were supposed to be, we sped off laughing without answering. Perhaps I should have answered to confuse him – maybe something like singing in a high-pitched voice, "You took a long time to see me, Lucille." Remember that song?

Occasionally while on night shift, in order to break the boredom, we would practice shooting. Sometimes we shot rabbits, coyotes, etc. Other times, we just set up a target in an isolated area and shot at the target. The police department only issued six bullets when they gave us our guns, so in order to enable target shooting, most of us carried reloaded ammunition which we either prepared ourselves or bought from another policeman who sold reloads.

The guns they issued were a joke: Webley brand .38 caliber six-shot revolvers. They were something right out of the remnants of the last world war and designed in the First World War; antiquated pieces of metal crap. The velocity on the issued Webley was about 620 feet per second – only about 150 feet per second faster than a .177 pellet gun. A 9mm pistol has a velocity of 1000 to 1300 feet per second. As a result, many of our guys either carried their own, more powerful handgun or a sawed-off shotgun in their brief cases.

One night shift we were practicing just outside the city limits at a target we set up about fifty or so feet away. The target was quite small, and I was missing it more than I was hitting it, so in frustration I threw the damn Webley at it. I missed again, but "oh what a feeling", and it just shows you how useless we thought our guns were. Had it been an individual I was shooting at, the Webley probably would not have been effective in taking him down.

In doing our nightly patrols we found a large field that seemed to be overrun with rabbits. Well now, this seemed like a good opportunity for some good old cowboy gun practice. I was in the passenger seat and my partner was driving. There was about an inch of snow in the field, so we could see a lot of rabbit footprints, and we did come across an occasional one here and there.

The idea that came to mind was to chase the rabbits with the police car. I had my gun out the passenger side window and was shooting at them while they were "torquing out" and trying to get away. It was pretty good entertainment for about fifteen or so minutes, but then we decided just to park and have a sleep in that field. Come morning when we woke up, we looked up and there was a development of town homes on top of the hill just above this field. "Oops!" We didn't notice that! We should have seen it when we were shooting or at least before we parked to sleep.

It turned out that it wasn't a field at all, but a golf course. The townhomes were overlooking the damn golf course!

Surely the noise of the gunfire had to get the attention of somebody, and if they looked down, they might have seen our police car in stunt mode playing chase and shoot the wild bunnies. It sure would have been funny if we got a call to investigate that complaint!

Another time we were just outside the city limits, and I saw some ducks floating on top of a pond about 150 feet from the road. I asked my partner to stop the car so I could have a shot at one of the ducks. He did so and I shot. Damned if the duck didn't fall over in the water. That was one shot I was quite proud of but "my bad" for aggravating animal lovers. My apologies, but things were really different back then, not at all like today.

One time I was working dayshift alone and was called to investigate a break and enter at a business in the northwest. I arrived to see the front window of the store was broken out. It was obviously the way the culprits had entered the premises. My job in handling the break-in consisted of writing a report that would be followed up by a detective unit to see if they could solve the crime. I got all the information from the storeowner: the location, the estimated time that the offense occurred, and anything else that could be pertinent in solving the crime.

When I was leaving, there were two young fellows outside walking by. I stopped them and checked their IDs and wrote down their names. We were taught that almost every time someone commits an offense at a location, for some reason or another, many will go back and have a look at the crime scene. This is particularly true with arsonists, but it also happens in cases like this. The reason I received a written commendation for this was because the detectives, after interviewing these two guys, were able to get them to confess to the crime. I was commended (written kudos) for doing my job.

Before a shift started, we would all line up for the daily parade. Basically, it's a piss poor inspection of your uniform and tools. Three lines totaling about 100 cops would hold up their billy clubs and handcuffs like we were in grade three. The staff sergeant would glance up and then read us the current lookout sheets. If you forgot your billy club, you just held up a finger of a glove, and from where he stood, it looked like a billy club.

One guy even forgot to put on his boots, so he stood in the back row in his slippers. He probably was drinking because I can't figure out how anyone could forget to put on their boots. Anyways, he got away with it and everyone who noticed covered for him because that behavior was condoned.

That night, the sergeant read an item on the lookout sheet that the detective division had entered. The detectives had driven through various parking lots of residential high rises in the downtown area and noticed a lot of fingerprints on the trunk of a rental car. It was a 1970 Chev Impala convertible license number "whatever". We were instructed to keep an eye out for that car because it was a rental unit with enough fingerprints on the trunk lid to suspect burglary involvement.

Later, the shift was coming to an end after my partner and I woke up from a couple of hours of sleep. It was time to head back to headquarters. On our way back, I spotted a red Chevrolet convertible approaching us in the opposite direction. A quick glance at the license plate made us realize this was the car the detectives were circulating.

We wheeled around, caught up to the car, and pulled it over. When I approached the vehicle, I noticed a pile of fur coats on the back seat. There were two male occupants in the front seat. When I questioned the driver, he said that they had just dropped off their girlfriends and they must have forgotten their coats. I could see sales tags on the coats, so I opened the back door to have a closer look and saw four fur coats. They all had sales tags from a well-known ladies clothing shop.

We made the occupants exit the car and placed them in the back of the police car while we investigated further. When I opened the trunk it was completely full of clothing as well, all from the same ladies clothing shop. The two were arrested for possession of stolen property, and it was learned that they did in fact break into the clothing shop that night to steal all of this clothing.

If I look back, it was excellent police work on the part of the detectives and we were alert enough to spot the car when passing it head on. Nothing like getting a written commendation for waking up in the morning and being rewarded for opening your eyes enough to read a license plate!

Another arrest that I received an commendation for occurred while walking a beat in a rough part of the city's east end. When you walk a beat you are expected to do a lot of door checking, so I went down the alley because the rear doors of businesses are the ones most likely to get broken into.

I wasn't fully concentrating on my job at the time. I was actually walking on the metal rails of the railroad track behind a warehouse and just balancing on the track as I walked. It wasn't much different than what a young child would do. Not that I was a young child, but when nobody is watching, you do whatever you feel like doing and that's what I felt like doing.

Each side of the railroad track was covered in loose gravel, so if I had been walking on the gravel like one would do normally, the noise would have been loud enough to alert the individual who had just broken into one of the buildings. He didn't hear me coming. I saw the door ajar so I went in slowly and quietly. He had no idea I was there when I yelled out, "What the hell are you doing in here?" I'm sure he damn near had a heart attack because he was crouched down, working on a safe, and he actually fell over. That made him very easy to catch! It meant another good arrest and another written commendation for good police work. It's always about the end result; not the theatrics or the wisdom involved.

While working in the south portion of the city, my partner and I were sleeping behind a service station. We had the windows partially open for fresh air because when a car is running and all the windows are up, it can lead to carbon monoxide poisoning. We left it running with the heat on while we slept. Once again we were not in our own area, but the service station had a number of cars parked behind it, so we could blend in and park there without being noticed.

"Without being noticed" is key here because not long after we were parked, we heard glass breaking in the front of the service station. We simply had to walk around to the front door to catch a guy who had broken in. He was really surprised because it appeared to him that we had arrived there on foot. Our particular area was quite a bit further south than that service station, so we just put in our report that while driving by we noticed an individual breaking in and quickly apprehended him.

There's that end result, once again. I'll take those commendations any way I can get them. Commendations back then were a big thing. They were official brownie points that stayed on your record for future advancement, and they were a pretty good thing to have on your record. In my case it would never have done any good because I was looking to get on the fire department.

I feel that although my past indicates I should have never been accepted on the police department, my record there was excellent. I was good at performing that job. Why, or how can I say that? It's because I used common sense rather than the rule book. I have known many people who use the rule book simply because they have no common sense. I never went against the grain of fellow workers, and my actions were acceptable because I accepted corruption as the "norm". I'm not saying my commendations were earned because I was a good cop, I got them simply for being in the right place at the wrong time on the clock of the criminal element.

One night on the City Police, my partner and I were driving to a police lunch station in a small satellite office. While on route, there was a German shepherd running around on the road in a confused state. My partner opened the back door of the police car, and when he called the dog, the damn thing jumped right in and sat down on the back seat.

Then we thought it would be quite funny if when we got to the lunch station, we took the German shepherd out of our car and put it in the back seat of one of the other police cars that were parked there. So that's what we did. I have to admit it looked pretty hilarious with the German shepherd sitting upright in the back seat patiently waiting. We could only imagine the surprised look on the faces of the two officers that went back to their car to find a dog sitting there. We decided to eat our lunch elsewhere to avoid blame. We later learned that they took the dog back to the station, and in the morning it was taken to the SPCA.

One fight I clearly remember was when I was driving an unmarked truck that was normally used for picking up stolen bicycles. I was in plainclothes. I had my gun tucked in my belt rather than in the holster because I was on a special duty surveillance mission. I saw an individual who appeared suspicious because he was parked in the commercial area I was watching. I approached him while he remained in his car, and when I identified myself as a policeman, he challenged me. I had forgotten to bring my badge wallet with me so I had no way of identifying myself. It was awkward.

I couldn't pull out my gun because that might have escalated the situation and could have gone very wrong. He wasn't breaking any laws so I was temporarily at a loss as to how to handle this situation. I botched that whole approach badly. He was convinced I was impersonating a cop. He got out of his car and put himself in an offensive position, which escalated things pretty quickly.

I clumsily showed him my handcuffs, but I still wasn't about to pull out my revolver. Then we tussled a bit until my gun fell out of my belt and slid across the pavement. That made things a lot more concerning, and I quickly retrieved it saying, "I had no reason to pull a gun on you but you haven't been very compliant so now it's come to this." I held my revolver down by my side. "Now show me some ID so I know who you are or should I call in for some assistance and charge you for assaulting a police officer?"

Then he was cooperative. I ran his name through the system using the truck radio and there was nothing on him. I let him go after recording his information in my note pad and accepted his excuse for being there. He had to pee and I interrupted him before he had the opportunity. I jokingly told him he was a hell of a fighter, full of piss and vinegar, but he should go and pee now to get rid of some of it. Then I went back to my observation spot.

Most police departments within Canada and the USA will give a courteous ""wave off" to other law-enforcement officers regardless of the force they belong to. In other words, they let each other go for minor offenses like speeding. This also applies to customs officers when stopped by state patrol, sheriffs, and other agencies. I know that from experience because I have been stopped for speeding by state patrol and small town city cops. Once they know that you are also a law enforcement officer, they send you on your way

However, one of the six tickets I gave out in my four years was to a "horseman". There was a line on the ticket that required you to list their occupation. I threw the ticket into the end–of-night ticket basket and a fellow cop picked it up. He gave me holy hell for ticketing an RCMP officer. (RCMP were called "horsemen" because they always show pictures of themselves up on a horse). When he finished reprimanding me, I said, " Hey, dumb ass! He isn't a fucking cop! He told me he was a cowboy and rounded up cattle on a horse. He gave me his occupation as 'horseman' when I asked for it. Understand?" He laughed and sort of apologized.

While patrolling on night shift my partner and I shot a rabbit. It was winter so the rabbit was white. We thought, "How cool it would be to follow a sergeant without being spotted." Why? To prank him with the rabbit.

The sergeant's car had a siren in the front center of the roof with a red strobe light just behind the siren. We were thinking of the Easter rabbit sitting on his two back feet with his other two feet held out in front of him. When the Sergeant stopped for coffee, we set the rabbit up, perching it in between the siren and the red light. It was winter so it was cold enough that the rabbit froze solid in that position. We parked across the street where we could see him, but he couldn't see us. WTF! Somehow he didn't notice, and he actually drove away with the rabbit up there! Can you imagine what the consequences of that picture on Facebook would be today? Even back then, our imaginations went wild thinking about the reaction of the public if they saw that. I have no idea how long it was before he found it, but I would have paid admission to have been there when he did.

Another night we were working in one of the poorer districts in the city. We got a call about a patron in the bar that was refusing to leave when requested to do so. When cops walk into a bar in uniform there's nothing but jeering and whistling, which usually gets the attention of almost everyone in the bar. We met up with the bouncer who took us over to the table where the unruly fellow was sitting. We politely asked him to leave the bar or we would have to arrest him.

He simply looked up at us and said, "I'm not going anywhere." A little strategy was needed here so we went off to the corner and told the bouncer that I would grab him by the hair and around the neck while my partner grabbed him by the arm and belt. The bouncer was just to assist us wherever he felt he could, hopefully to grab his other arm. Then we would run for the door dragging the man behind us so we could get out quickly to avoid a potentially volatile situation. Often times when they are liquored up, a crowd will rise to the occasion to help a friend when they feel the odds are stacked in favor of the cops.

We put the plan into action, and I grabbed the guy by the hair and around the neck while my partner grabbed his belt and arm. The bouncer grabbed his other arm, and we ran for the door to get him outside. Once outside, he went into fighting mode. He wasn't a small man, being over six feet tall and probably weighing 200 pounds. After fighting with him for what seemed like five minutes, I was ready to throw up. We finally got him subdued and in the backseat of our police car. I jumped in with him in case he got unruly again even though he was now cuffed.

By that time he had calmed down and I was finally was able to get my breath. He looked at me and said "Shit! You guys are out of shape!" We never charged him with obstruction or resisting arrest because he calmed down so much he was now friendly. The next morning he appeared before a judge for being drunk and disorderly.

I went to his court appearance because I wanted to make sure he didn't comment about how or why he had bruises on his face. If he mentioned any perceived abuse to the judge it might have caused some report writing, but it didn't happen. What a relief!

Another time on City Police, we were alerted by the federal cops that they were in a car chase and the individual was headed into our city. They were requesting assistance by way of a roadblock to stop this individual.

The usual procedure for setting up a roadblock was to block all but one lane on the highway to give the offender a place to go rather than smashing into the police cars.

We ignored that protocol. We thought it would be more interesting to watch him slam into the police cars, so we blocked all four lanes of the highway. We could hear the siren approaching but we didn't notice a side road between us and the approaching offender.

The guy slammed on his brakes and made a right-angle turn at the same time at an unbelievable rate of speed. The feds that were following him tried the same maneuver, but they crashed into the ditch and their siren remained on and was actually stuck on the highest wailing tone. It was just too funny really. CRASH! Whhhhhhhhhhhhhhhhhrrrr.

We all ran for our cars like a bunch of keystone cops and drove all over the neighborhood on almost every street, crisscrossing one another chasing this seemingly phantom guy. Nobody actually saw him until one car finally cut him off. He did try to drive off again, but the car that found him made a quick and successful maneuver to stop him. When the police officer got him out of the car and handcuffed him, it was the first time anyone knew there were three terrified passengers in his vehicle. What was really surprising was that shots were fired during the chase. No wonder they were terrified! Everyone who fired a shot was asked to submit a report, but no reports were submitted. The evidence that shots were fired was obvious because there were three bullet holes in the trunk of his car. It was never known who fired them.

One could assume that the feds fired on him because I didn't believe our .38 Webleys could have penetrated the trunk. It was either the feds or else one of our cops was using his personal gun. It was later learned that the reason the fellow was running from the police was because he had beer in his car. He had just applied for a job with the feds and had been accepted so he didn't want to compromise that.

One of my pals on the police was a detective who I'll call Carl. He used to have sort of a "tit for tat" dispute going on with one of the chauffeurs in the garage where a lot of police cars were parked. The chauffeur got on Carl's nerves very quickly, so Carl devised a plan to put an end to all the kibitzing. He told the chauffeur to knock it off before he elevated his actions to a serious situation. The chauffeur took his warning very lightly and mouthed off back to him with a smart-ass remark.

Carl had previously put blanks in his firearm with the intention of firing it at the chauffeur to silence him once and for all. So just as he planned, he pulled out his firearm and aimed at the chauffeur who was about 50 feet away and fired off two rounds at him. The chauffeur thought the rounds were live and jumped to the ground. After realizing he had been duped, he was extremely angry so he reported the incident to the duty inspector.

As I said, our superiors on the police department pretty much always had your back in those days. I assumed that Carl was called into the office and given the old "don't do that again" lecture and that was the end of it. It was so damn funny because I thought the chauffeur almost pissed his pants.

One night shift, my partner and I were driving through our area. My partner said he saw somebody skulking around between some campers and motorhomes that were on a recreation vehicle sales lot. I drove around the block and parked on a side street so we could walk unnoticed into the RV lot and investigate. We were almost right beside one of the motorhomes when the door flung open and a naked woman came running out followed by a naked man chasing her.

What the hell? They were both giggling and apparently they didn't see us because they ran over to and entered another motorhome a few spots over and closed the door behind them. We knocked on the door and heard some scampering inside for a few seconds, and then the naked man answered the door surprised as hell to see two cops standing there. "What's going on here, buddy?" we asked.

"Get some clothes on and come out here so you can explain what in the heck you and the lady are doing in these motor homes and bring some identification out with you." "Well that's a problem," he said. "Our clothes are in another motorhome."

"In that case, you come out and I'll go with you to your clothing. You can dress and bring the lady's clothing back with you so she can dress and we can talk to her."

My partner stayed at the door where the lady was, and I went back with man so he could dress. He told me that this was his sales lot, and he and the lady were just having some fun. I wrote down his particulars and once he gave the lady's clothing to her we compared their stories. She apparently worked at the RV place as well, so after taking notes we left.

Thinking back, it would have been a lot more interesting if I had asked the lady to get her clothing first, then come back and see the man to compare their stories. Sometimes, appropriateness just seems to be so boring.

Our city jail cells were like most you see on TV with the exception of the drunk tanks, which were usually cesspools by morning considering all the puking and pissing that was done throughout the night by the drunks locked in there. In the morning, the cops that worked there usually solicited one or two prisoners to wash out the drunk tanks. There were small cells as well for longer staying patrons. Those cells were used to allow easy access to prisoners who had active or upcoming court dates rather than bringing them in daily from far-away correctional facilities.

They were all fed toast and jam in the morning. It was delivered in a couple of brown-paper grocery bags by a caterer. Cleanliness was usually not a consideration. Lunches were similar – bulk sandwiches piled up on large trays and most of them did not go untouched by others. Refreshments came in pitchers to fill paper cups. Supper came on paper plates piled on top of each other.

There was one multi-prisoner day cell, but it only had one stainless steel toilet, which when in use was viewed by all. If you've ever thought about a life of crime this could be a deterrent, especially when trying to have a crap and wipe your ass with twenty convicts watching you.

We had a call one evening to attend an attempted suicide at a downtown high-rise. A lady that lived on the 20th floor threatened to commit suicide. This wasn't the first time I'd been called to this particular residence. I was called at least twice before and other members had been called there before as well.

Once again, we took her into custody under the Mental Health Act and brought her down the elevator to the police car. For some reason, this time the woman thought it was a good idea to jump into the passenger seat in the front of our car. My seat! Asking, then telling her to get out was unsuccessful. She flat-out refused. My only option seemed to be to call the policewoman on duty which was routine when dealing with difficult women or juveniles. At that time, men and women cops were not partnered together in police cars.

When the policewoman got there, she simply yanked the lady out of the car and threw her into our back seat. That is something I could've done, but when spectators are watching it's always better for a woman to roughhouse another woman. For some stupid reason, people get pissed off when a man does it. Go figure!

I was frustrated and angry with this lady by that time, so on the way to the hospital to check her into the mental ward, I told her we were getting tired of attending her repeated suicide attempts. I know that's cold, but you can only take so much before you lose your temper. I think I failed my empathy class or I mistakenly enrolled in the apathy class instead. Sadly, she did jump twenty floors to a very unpleasant ending. I'm quite glad I was not on duty that night.

Talk about a staff turnover, when I started on the force I was given a number. I was number 495. Four years later when I quit, I was 339. They did another renumber exercise a month after I left. Had I stayed an extra month my number would have been 227. Doing the math translates to 268 cops that quit or retired in a four year period. More than half the force. No wonder they hired me with a partial grade-10 education

Strangely enough, after quitting the police I had serious regrets for more than 10 years. The excitement on that job created high adrenaline rushes and I really missed that.

Part Seven:
Joined The Fire Department

AFTER FOUR YEARS with the police, I finally got a response from the fire department, but I had to do a physical endurance test in order to pass. The test was pretty extreme. I had to put a 50-pound sack on my shoulders and run along a plank, balance on it while walking without falling off, and then throw the weight off some 50 feet away and run back through an obstacle course. The course had me go under some ropes and over fences. The finale was to race all the other candidates who were competing. I was under the impression that they only took the top six of those racing. I put more effort into that than I thought I had in my body.

I was determined I was going to win. There was only one individual in front of me near the finish line, but going into the last lap close to the finish, he slipped on some water and fell. I was able to get past him and I came in first. For the next test, they put breathing apparatus on us with tanks and masks, but they blacked out the masks so we couldn't see. For the last test, we had to find our way around the inside of a building and blindly locate a stuffed dummy. Once found, I was supposed to take it outside if I could find the damn door. I did okay because I made it in good time and was hired.

On one of my first nights after joining the City Fire Department, we attended a heart attack call as first responders to give the ambulance crew time to get there. The subject was lying on the kitchen floor in a pile of vomit while his wife looked on. She was only too happy to step aside and let us take over. As the rookie, I was instructed to wipe up the vomit to make the working conditions a little more pleasant, so to speak. That was a little bit gut-wrenching because the stench of vomit has a tendency to activate the gag reflex in people. It was effective; believe me.

This individual turned out to be a success story because we put a resuscitator on him quickly and did heart compressions to keep him alive until the ambulance crew got there. I only mention this case because this individual later sent a heartwarming letter to our fire hall thanking the crew for helping to save his life. It was a really a great feeling to hear from him.

I was with the city fire department for only three years. Some of our calls were quite morbid. One incident that clearly comes to mind was attending a traffic accident on a busy highway. There was a serious collision involving two passenger cars. The police were already in attendance when we rolled up in the fire truck to extricate a body that was awkwardly stuck behind and under the steering wheel. He was definitely dead. I distinctively remember that. After prying the driver's door open and then lifting the steering column up from where the windshield was, he fell out of the car and his head hit the pavement with a thump, like a watermelon.

Worse yet, his skull was only half there, and what I think was brain matter dumped out onto the pavement. Psychologically that was pretty hard to take because the individual was about the same age as my dad and that's all I could think about. This was probably somebody's dad and I thought how horrible it would've been had he been mine.

Another call was to a steakhouse type of restaurant that was on the second floor of one of the commercial buildings on the highway. We usually beat the ambulance to medical calls and in this case they took a while. When we went upstairs, the restaurant staff pointed us in the direction of the men's washroom and said there was an individual who was lying on the floor in one of the cubicles.

Sure enough, there was a very large fellow lying on the floor preventing us from getting easy access to him because the cubicle door opened inwards. He was too fat for us to get the door open easily and was pretty much stuck between the toilet and the door.

His pants were down and there was shit all over him because he appeared to have had a heart attack and died in the middle of his dump. We struggled to move him over enough to get the door open and then dragged him out into the main part of the bathroom. There we applied the resuscitator but to no avail. That created a real mess because now we had shit all over the resuscitator and at least three of us were adorned with his poop.

The guy weighed about 350 pounds and was not an easy man to move, but we managed to get him on a fire department canvas stretcher. Now we had to get him down the stairs. It was a long stairway, probably about 18 steps, while carrying a 350-pound weight on that stretcher. Two firefighters were on one side, one on the other, one at the bottom, and I was at the top during this task.

There was no other way to get him out. The man's wife was anxiously standing by at the top of the stairs along with another couple whom they had been dining. They were waiting to see how the husband would fare through all this. We knew he was dead because he no longer had a pulse, but it wasn't our practice to tell people their loved ones had perished. It is something that is very difficult to do. We thought we would get him in the ambulance quickly and send him on route to the hospital where a doctor could pronounce his death.

That's when things got interesting. Going down the stairs, the guy on the left side caved because the stretcher was sloped at almost a 45-degree angle to descend the stairway, and it was too much for them to hold. All of a sudden, their side dropped and the guy rolled off the stretcher and was lying on the stairs like a huge blob of play-dough.

We immediately set the stretcher down on the steep angle of the stairs, and the guys struggled to roll his humongous body back onto it. His wife was standing at the top of the stairs behind us. Since I was the firefighter at the top when he fell, I opened my duty coat and held it out like Batman to try and block her vision and hide the slip-up while the others fought to get him back onto the stretcher.

I have no idea what was going through his wife's mind at that time or if she even saw it. They managed to scoop him back onto the stretcher, and we completed the journey down the stairs. Finally, we managed to get him onto the ambulance gurney which now was just outside the door at the bottom. Luckily the ambulance was in place.

We put him in the ambulance and closed the door. We told his wife that she could not accompany him because they were still giving him CPR in hopes of resuscitating him. She was instructed to go to the hospital for a follow-up. It was a very long evening full of stress and emotion and ended in sadness and drama, all covered with shit.

In going to another heart attack call, we started resuscitation on an individual before the ambulance crew arrived. The victim lived alone but managed to call for help. By the time we arrived, he had passed. Once the ambulance arrived, we helped them load the body onto the gurney. Then they came back to get some more information to complete their paperwork. However, they acted in haste because they neglected to fully close the back doors of the ambulance. They also neglected to lock the gurney onto the floor locks.

By now you may have guessed what happened next. They got back into the ambulance, put it in gear, and took off. All of a sudden, the back doors flew open and the gurney with the body on it came flying out and bounced onto the ground. It fell over sideways with the body still strapped in place on it. I yelled at them that their cargo just took a hike, but by then, they had already figured that out. There didn't seem to be anyone around that might have been related to the corpse, but it sure got everyone's attention and of course was quite embarrassing for those ambulance attendants.

For information sake, the city fire department had a routine procedure while attending a fire when a pumper truck was dispatched. The hydrant man would jump off as soon as the truck stopped at the fire hydrant and do his thing. On route to a fire, the attack crew used to stand on the rear platform of the fire truck. There were no crew cab trucks back then and sometimes things got interesting. The driver would go through red lights if he could do it safely, but many motorists simply don't hear sirens or see red flashing lights.

In one instance where a vehicle failed to yield, the pump driver briefly had to come to a stop. The hydrant man knew that upon arriving at a fire he could jump off, grab a hose and run for the hydrant to anchor it. However, from the back of the truck he couldn't always see if we had arrived. You guessed it! He jumped off when the driver came to a quick stop at the light because of traffic that failed to yield. Then before he could even grab the hose from the truck, the driver took off leaving him behind at the intersection. He ran after the truck at a full gallop trying to catch up.

There was a push-button switch on the back, and if the driver hears three rings from that push button, it means stop. It was pushed three times, so the truck stopped 25 yards past the intersection. The embarrassed hydrant man caught up and got back on the truck while the rest of us almost fell off laughing.

One time, there was a fire in a ground-floor apartment. The apartment was full of smoke, and flames were seen deeper inside. The couple that rented the apartment was outside waiting for us and said their baby was still inside in his new crib. On this occasion I wasn't driving, so I got my breathing apparatus on quickly as did the nozzle man. We entered the building as soon as possible to look for the crib, hosing the flames as we moved through the apartment.

We found the crib quickly and the baby was in it, but he was lifeless and badly burned. I picked him up and ran to the exit. Other crews arrived by then, and I handed the baby off to one of them. The guy I gave the baby to immediately handed him off to another firefighter because the stench of burned flesh was more than he could take and he felt he needed to vomit.

I had my breathing apparatus on so I couldn't smell the burned flesh. I was ready to punch the baby's father though because all I could hear him say was he had just bought that baby crib brand new and now it was burned. Later in my career I learned that his behavior was probably due more to shock than to ignorance, but I did not realize it back then.

I remember one night while on duty, the fire department guys were all having a couple of beers while lying in their beds and having a bullshit session. The captain and lieutenant slept in a different dormitory close to the alarm room, so if an alarm came in they were handy to take information from the dispatcher while the rest of the crew was gearing up.

They wouldn't have been too happy to find out we were drinking beer, but alcohol consumption while at the fire department did happen on occasion. We usually enjoyed wine around Christmas when we were having a turkey dinner amongst the crew. The alcohol consumed at those particular dinners was usually minimal, and the members were pretty careful about tipping back too many. Occasionally, one or two might have consumed more than they should have, but we just had to make sure those guys weren't the ones operating the pump or any another fire apparatus.

We played poker quite a bit to pass the evenings. Some of those games yielded some firefighters high returns and others lost paychecks. The chief got wind of that when one of the wives complained to him that her husband had lost most of his paycheck playing poker. It was easy to do when some of the pots had over a hundred bucks in them. The chief thought he'd put an end to the gambling by prohibiting playing poker with money. So instead of playing with cash, we substituted poker chips that had monetary value. Not much changed, but most halls switched to penny value chips. I thought it was a shame that it took one of the wives to exercise some common sense to try to put a stop to stupidity.

Most of the time, I drove the pumper truck or another vehicle, but occasionally I was on the back of the truck. Your assigned position varied. One of the halls I was stationed in had three fire trucks inside a two-bay fire hall – a pumper, a tanker, and an aerial ladder truck. One day when I was driving out of the hall responding to a call with the aerial ladder, the tanker truck was parked between my aerial rig and the pumper truck on the other side.

A tanker truck is a water-carrying truck capable of carrying 1000 gallons of water or more, and it is used in locations where fire hydrants are not abundant. They can be tricky to drive, even when outfitted with baffles that prevent the water from sloshing around front to back, or side to side with enough weight to affect the handling of the truck.

Unbeknownst to me, the driver of the tanker truck opened his door fully while getting in, which compromised my exit from the hall with the aerial ladder. The door of the tanker caught the side of the aerial ladder and rendered the tanker door somewhat inoperable. All these trucks are big enough that when you have a little accident like that, you don't generally feel it as it happened in this case. The tanker truck continued on to the fire location and when he got there, the driver got out and told me that I caught his door while leaving the hall.

The blame would be on him because when I leave the hall I watch to make sure that I'm not taking off the side or bottom of the roll up doors. You don't expect something to appear inside from nowhere that obstructs your exit. You should not have to watch out for doors opening against your truck. It's like opening a car door into traffic. But no big deal. Both he and I had to write reports on how this happened and how it could have been prevented for future reference. It wasn't hard to explain, but I recommended that they either get a bigger fire hall with enough bays for every truck or hire thinner firefighters so they don't have to open the doors so wide while entering their trucks.

Occasionally the captain would take out an entire crew on practice driving sessions. Often times it was just to break boredom, and we usually stopped at an ice-cream place to get ourselves ice-cream cones. The truck I normally drove was in for servicing, and as a spare they gave me a 1948 model truck as a replacement vehicle while the servicing was being done. The captain thought it would be a good idea for me to take the crew on a practice ride to familiarize me with the aged operating procedure of this old fire truck. It seemed like a good idea, and the crew jumped on the back. The captain and I were in the cab and away we went.

The shift linkage on an old truck like that was in the neighborhood of 23 feet long, consisting of a number of combined links. As a result, when I stopped for a red light, the linkage jammed. It somehow stuck between first and reverse gear and would neither go forward nor backward. We had to call for a tow truck to come and get the truck. We also had to wait for another truck to pick us up at a very busy intersection, on a very busy highway, on a downhill slope towards the highway. It got to be quite embarrassing. Imagine five firefighters in their firefighting gear on the road standing around their truck, which was stalled at an intersection blocking a lane.

In order to facilitate easier towing I dumped the water tank to lighten the load so a stream was also running down to the main highway. This attracted even more attention but made it look more like a breakdown. I'm pretty sure it wasn't my fault that the linkage locked up. Nevertheless, I tried to mingle with the other firefighters so that it would be harder to identify me as the driver to members of the public who were watching. The truck and I were both made in 1948. In my case it was a good year. The truck, not so much!

For some training in the fire department, there was a practice building that was about four stories high and made of cement block with steel windows. The instructors would light fires behind the steel windows, and we had to rappel down the outside of the building on a rope. While we were doing that, we had to avoid hitting the closed windows by rappelling past them. To do it successfully, you had to kick off the wall above the doors and slide down past them to keep from getting burned.

I have to admit I sucked at that, and often when I rappelled down that building, I would stop too soon and expose myself to the fire inside. That really burned my ass! (Just an expression.) Fortunately I was fast enough to kick myself away from the window again by straddling it and sliding down a little bit more to eventually reach the ground floor.

Another one of the practice sessions involved putting the aerial ladder up to about 75 feet in the air but angled off just slightly. A water monitor (huge water nozzle) was attached to the top of the aerial ladder and the hose was charged. When I opened the nozzle, the force of the water pressure made that ladder torque backwards at least six feet, and when closing the nozzle, it would swing back to its original position. I found that to be amusing, so I turned the nozzle on and off just to make the ladder swing. (Not a recommended training practice).

Believe it or not, one of the newer firefighters up on that ladder immediately came down after his turn and resigned from the fire department. He told the instructors that he had the strongest urge to jump when he was up there. No one argued with him because the decision to quit was a decision that he made on his own, and one that probably saved the fire department some embarrassment in the future should he someday decide he was really going to do it.

At this particular city fire department, we had many groups of school children come to our fire halls. We were instructed to take them on mini tours of the hall. One of the thrills for the kids was to watch a firefighter slide down a pole. Most fire halls are ground level buildings, but some are two stories with the living quarters upstairs. The living quarters were never part of the tour probably because if the public knew we slept in beds at night, some objection might surface, so why advertise it?

Anyway, when I worked in a fire hall that had a pole, the kids loved to see a fireman slide down. I enjoyed that because the first time I slid down for them they smiled so I said, "Now, do you want me to do that again, but the next time I'll stop halfway down?"

Of course they wanted to see that. You might not have thought that was possible, but it is and it is quite easy. Using your leg and arm muscles for tension, you can stop dead on a slippery brass fire pole and surprise the heck out of people. It always brought on applause.

What didn't bring on applause was a gag I pulled on a group of preschoolers. I thought it would be funny, but my humor is sometimes clouded, and this was one of those days. The group of kids I was giving a tour to were about five years old on average. I was taking them around the fire truck and showing them what was in every compartment on the truck and answering a few questions while doing so.

Then I asked them if they had ever seen any of the fire department pull boxes that were situated in their schools and around the neighborhood. I explained to them that people should only pull one of those fire alarm switches if there actually was a fire, and sometimes bad people will pull one because they think it's funny. I made it clear that it was wrong to activate a false alarm and it wasn't funny. Then I asked them if they knew what would happen to them if they did initiate a false alarm.

I didn't give them time to answer because I immediately opened a compartment on the truck that they hadn't seen the contents of yet. In that compartment I had placed a mannequin head with a full head of hair on it. I pulled it out by the hair and held the head up above them and said, "This is what will happen to you!" Within seconds I realized it was not as funny as I thought it would be. The kids appeared shocked, and their adult chaperones were clearly unimpressed. I probably should have been disciplined for it, but the chaperones didn't complain and my captain didn't see it. I was lucky and got away with it.

During my three years with the big city fire department, we had a fair-sized fire in a cabaret. It was badly burned inside, but there were still dozens of bottles of hard liquor that hadn't been broken. Perfect! We had two water filled portable hand pump fire extinguishers on the truck for putting out small smoldering spots, so we dumped the water out and filled those extinguishers with liquor. Then we let the bottles fall and break with the others. We couldn't let the captain know what we had done so we had to pretend our pump cans were empty. We put them back on the truck until we could transfer the liquor into suitable containers without getting caught.

When we got back to the hall, one of the guys went to get some groceries. He picked up six gallons of distilled water, dumped out the water, then brought the empty one-gallon containers into the hall, two at a time. While the rest of the crew distracted the captain, we transferred the booze into the plastic jugs and put them into each of the firefighters' cars. Then we refilled the extinguishers with water.

It was risky because the time it took to do all this was sketchy. If the liquor was left in the extinguishers, all hell would break loose if someone on the next shift had to use one of them. It turned out to be a bad idea anyway because the alcohol was a mixture of various types, and it wasn't all that pleasant to drink.

I put my gallon jug in the cupboard with my booze stash, and my wife almost dumped it out thinking there was something wrong with the distilled water because it wasn't clear. I had to tell her what it was and where it came from. That brought on one of her lectures about irresponsibility.

Remember when I told you police take care of their own! Many police officers also included firefighters as "brothers of a sort" (both being emergency services workers), and one night while a firefighter, I was pulled over by a cop for speeding. He could smell liquor on me so he asked me, "How much have you had to drink tonight?"

I said, "Six or seven beers."

My wife was with me so he asked, "Has your wife also been drinking?"

I said, "Yes, she has but not as much as me."

He then crouched down to look at her and said, "How much have you had to drink tonight, ma'am?"

She said while slurring, "Five or six beers." I almost burst out laughing because she admitted having only one less drink than me. He shook his head and asked how far we were from home. We were pretty close so he let us continue without any consequences. We made it home just fine. I think I had more experience driving drunk than she did sober anyway, but I sure didn't want the cop to know that.

A call out to a fire always got your adrenaline up simply because you never knew what you were about to get into. The department had an intercom system in place in every fire hall. It was operated by the dispatcher. It was very loud, and when you were in a deep sleep (say at 4:00 a.m.) and it went off, your heartbeat immediately elevated. In order to get your attention, the system was designed to alert you before the dispatcher spoke over the intercom. A horn similar to a car horn would blast. Then you needed to listen carefully. The horn blasts were each about two seconds long.

One blast meant: Notification – not a call to action – just information.

Two blasts meant: Small fire or accident call – only involving your particular hall.

Three blasts meant: At least two fire halls to attend a big fire.

Four blasts meant: Rescue or medical call – ambulances may be delayed.

Rookie firefighters usually suffered some form of prank or mild hazing. One day I had a plan to prank one of them. I got the go ahead from the others in our dorm to set up a car horn under his bed activated by a battery charger with an extension cord going back to my bed. I was going to plug in a second extension cord attached to a wall socket and join the two together once he went to sleep. While waiting for him to go to sleep, I fell asleep.

I woke up at about 2:00 a.m. and plugged the extensions together for about ten seconds. The horn blasted! The poor rookie didn't know what to do. It scared the hell out of others in the room as well.

He said afterward, "I heard the horn blast, but it was only one blast and for so long I thought it was a super bad emergency. I jumped into my gear, and when I looked back at you guys you were all still in bed laughing. I just thought, WTF is going on? But figured I'd been had pretty quickly. You bastards!"

Another prank was devised when we were playing cards near the end of the evening just before going to bed, We created a phony argument where I accused another firefighter of engaging in hanky-panky with my wife. Remember this was all an act. I stormed out of the lunchroom calling him a few derogatory names. He stayed in the lunchroom until the rookie went to bed because we all slept in the same dorm except for the two officers.

Once he knew the rookie was about ready to crawl under the covers, he entered the dorm and went to his locker. As soon as he got to his locker, I immediately called him a few more names and said, "I'LL KILL YOU, YOU SOB". As soon as I said that I brandished a pistol and fired a shot at him. The rookie was terrified and jumped down onto the floor out of my sight. He got up as soon as the laughter erupted at which time I showed him my starter pistol. Got him good!

We had a fire on the second floor of an industrial building that was pretty intense. We knocked it down from the outside for the most part with a two-and-a-half-inch line on a ground monitor nozzle. Once it was knocked down to the point where it looked like it was mostly smoke, I entered with another firefighter who was at the nozzle. I was a step or two behind him. I had been in there quite awhile and had exhausted my air supply. When that happens with breathing apparatus, an alarm bell rings for a couple of minutes before the tank completely empties. It's telling you that you are soon out of air.

I started back but my tank ran out completely before I got out, so in order to breathe with less smoke I disconnected the hose from the air tank and put it under my arm inside my coat to eliminate most of the smoke.

Smoke rises and the air is clearer near to the ground, so in order to find my way out, I had to crawl along the floor following the one-and-a-half-inch 'hand line' hose to guide my way out. It was stressful, but I made it because I had remembered that trick of removing the hose from the regulator as we had been trained to do. I'm not sure which was worse though – the B.O. from my armpit or the smoke.

After joining the fire department I quickly figured out that if you didn't have a part-time job, you would have a drinking problem. I believe I had both, but you really needed something to do with six out of every eight days off year round.

I had a few part-time jobs while working as a firefighter. One of my jobs was at a big department store, driving a truck and delivering furniture. The trucks were five-ton trucks, so you needed a class C license to drive them and all firefighters had class C licenses. (Now known as a class 3). Almost all of the drivers in that delivery warehouse were firefighters because the company knew who was off shift on what days and who wasn't, so usually I got a lot of part-time work from them.

A while later, after constantly applying for a job at the armored car company, my efforts finally came to fruition. I was hired as a part-time driver to pick up money. That job filled more time on my days off, so my days were busier. During horse race season, I would often drive the armored car through pedestrian traffic on the exhibition grounds in order to gain access to the racetrack where we picked up the proceeds from the races. We were told if anyone tried to hijack the truck and you had to shoot them, the company would give you a monetary reward.

People walking through the exhibition grounds were not cognizant of a big armored truck almost crawling up their asses at the slowest of speeds. Honestly, I could have pushed them out of the way with my truck bumper most of the time. I didn't, but I tried to get close enough to them to scare the shit out of them when I hit the horn right behind their ears. I found out those trucks are equipped with sirens.

Horseplay in the armored truck garage was interesting. We fired a shot at the truck window to see if the claim of bullet proof was accurate. It was! The .38 caliber bullet chipped a bulls-eye circle on the side window, but it didn't penetrate the glass. I think a .357 bullet might have made it through, but the revolvers issued to armored car employees back then were .38's. However, you can shoot a

.38 caliber bullet in a .357 handgun, but a .357 bullet in a .38 caliber gun can destroy it, cause it to blow up in your hand, or even kill you, so we didn't try.

Another of the part-time jobs that I applied for during my years on fire departments was as a bill collector, credit checker, and repo agent. One of my duties was to interview people who lived next door to individuals applying for credit to verify occupancy and the character of individuals seeking loans. In order to do that, I needed a suit to look respectable. But perhaps in that jacket and pants, respectable wasn't the right word for my appearance. Pimp would have been more suitable! I bought those flashy clothes from a big department store and only wore them a few times before realizing stalking people by questioning their neighbors was not my gig. I returned the suit, got my money back, and then quit that job.

Another part time gig while on the city fire department involved buying a few cars from an representative at a finance company. Sometimes you get them at a good price and sometimes you get screwed. I bought a 68 Buick Wildcat and a 68 Datsun 510 from that company. The Wildcat was a beautiful car and sold promptly for a respectable profit. The Datsun appeared to be a nice car too. However, the interior probably had a dead body in it for a long enough time to absorb the stench of a rotted carcass. When I bought the car it was a cool cloudy day and there was no smell. When it warmed up outside, the smell was gross. Whooa boy! This one was going to be hard to sell.

We took our wives out to supper using that car and had to open all the windows so the stench was partially neutralized. We finally sold it by telling potential buyers I worked until 7:00 p.m. so they wouldn't be able to test drive it until I got home. Then I put in a few air fresheners and with the cooler evening air, a buyer came through. Our motto was, "There's an ass for every seat." It was nice to see the taillights of that one driving away.

I partnered with my friend on these two vehicles. My reason for partnering was that I needed someone to drive and assist me in repossessing a car. The representative from the finance company knew I had an interest in repossessing vehicles. He asked me if I wanted to go to a city an hour or two away and repossess a Chevy station wagon. I eagerly accepted the assignment. I talked my friend into going with me. Besides, if we faced any physical altercations, two is a better number to overcome the odds than one.

The car seemed to be pretty solid and in good condition, so when we got back I asked the finance rep how much his company needed to get out of it and I bought the car. Working with a finance company was new territory for me. It turned out all right. Within a few days I sold it for what I paid plus an additional trade of a 500CC Triumph Trophy motorcycle. I damn near killed myself on that bike because back then, British bikes put the foot brake on the left and the toe shift on the right, which is opposite to Japanese and American motorcycles.

I roared down the street towards a busy cross street and, by habit, attempted to stop using the foot brake by pushing down on the toe shift. I almost went into traffic. Fortunately, I figured it out in time to stop. Yes, there is a hand brake, but if it's the only one that works, and you brake too hard, going too fast, you will regret it. That was the last British bike I ever owned and I've owned 23 motorcycles.

I also worked part-time for a locksmith changing locks on houses and apartment buildings. I was working in a fifty-unit apartment building which was under renovation when the building manager asked me if I wanted to buy one of the bar fridges they were replacing. "How much?"

"Fifty bucks."

"How many do you have?"

"Fifty," he said.

I said, "I'll buy them all, but I only want to pay $25 each for them."

"Deal, he said.

My boss and I took them all to my house and put them in my basement. Some needed serious cleaning but most were in pretty good condition. My friend Rick came over because I told him that ten of them were not working. I turned them upside down because I thought that the Freon in them wasn't circulating. He only looked at two them and then said, "They do work better if you turn them on you know!" Damn! I didn't notice the control switch inside.

My boss partnered up with me, and we both put ads in the paper asking $50 each for them. We sold them all in less than two weeks. In fact while I went to my firefighter job, I put three down the hallway in the house and one at the front door, so when my wife sold one she could pull another one to the door. I placed them on furry mats so she could drag them across the hardwood floor easily.

We advertised only one because if we advertised fifty everyone would haggle. A couple of people didn't want to pay $50 and said, "There is another one for sale a few blocks from here that we're going to look at so will you take $35?" Nope. They left, and we laughed because we knew the other fridge was one of ours as well. I phoned my boss and said, "Another cheap ass is coming your way." He did the same when someone tried to lowball him on the ones he had.

While I was working at the fire department, my wife and I enjoyed a good social life. Onetime, my good friend and part-time locksmith boss and I, with our wives, went out to for supper and a movie. After the movie we decided that it would be nice to go for a swim. We went by our respective homes and collected our bathing suits and off we went again.

My wife's parents lived in a townhouse in a development in the southwest. Part of their rental agreement was that they were permitted to use the swimming pool in one of the other buildings adjoined to the underground parking garage. We could have knocked on her parents' door and asked if we could borrow the key to go for a swim, but it was about midnight so that didn't seem to be a viable option. Besides, my boss, the locksmith that I worked for part-time, was very proficient at opening locks without a key.

We parked in the underground parkade adjacent to the pool, and he picked the lock. Then we went into the men's change room to put on bathing suits while our wives were in the ladies' change room. To our surprise, there was a lady in the men's change room. She was about our age, and she was totally naked. It didn't seem to bother her, but she did notice that our eyes were locked on to her boobs.

She noticed our perverted staring and made the comment, "The human body is nothing to be ashamed of." We agreed but kept staring at her until she left the change room naked and joined two guys who were already in the pool, but they were wearing swim trunks. We had our trunks on by then as well and jumped into the deep end with her to feast our eyes some more while treading water.

Our wives were at the shallow end of the pool so after treading water until we couldn't keep it up any longer (no pun intended), we swam over and pointed the naked chick out to them. Once we did that, they didn't feel like swimming anymore. Who would have guessed? So we left.

Another evening we were at the home of the same couple socializing, when they introduced us to a new drink – the "Russian Nikolaschka", which was comprised of a double shot of vodka, espresso coffee, a lemon slice, and sugar. The concoction is consumed by putting the lemon, sugar, and coffee in your mouth before taking a shot of vodka.

I had quite a few of those that night. In fact, I had so many I couldn't even get my boots on so my wife and my buddy helped me and then he walked me out to my truck. I started getting a little belligerent so rather than put up with my unpredictable behavior, he opened the tailgate of my pick-up and told me to lie down in there until my wife got me home. We only lived about half a mile from them, but when she was driving down the road, I stood up in the back of the pick-up truck without her noticing and took a few steps towards the open tailgate. I walked out of the moving truck onto the road.

Luckily, I was so drunk that I never injured myself at all. It was winter and the snow on the road provided a soft landing. However, I had just purchased a brand-new expensive leather jacket about a week before, and it was damaged in the fall. I viewed that as my punishment for being a bad boy that day.

We had a party at our house one afternoon with quite a few guests. It was hot and sunny all day. We BBQ'd outside and got severe sunburns. The next day something happened that made us decide to move to a milder climate. It friggin' snowed that night, and I had to shovel my sidewalk the next morning. That was the last straw! The weather in that city was nasty and unpredictable. We put our house up for sale, I quit the City Fire Dept. and we moved. We profited enough on the sale to pay cash for a house in a smaller city with a warmer climate and moved.

That was the first time I retired. Retirement didn't pan out very well because evidently we needed money to live on! I applied at a well-known life and disability insurance company for a position as a sales representative.

My dad had his own insurance business in that city, which was one of the reasons we chose to live there. He offered me a position in his office, but I wanted to make my own way in the world so I refused. In hindsight that would have been a very smart thing to do but "water under the bridge". The terms of my employment with that life insurance company were to receive wages for the first two months while being trained by an experienced agent, and then work on a commission-only basis.

The agent they sent out to train me instructed me to mail out as many handouts as possible to generate clients to buy life or disability insurance. I took his advice very seriously, and I mailed out over 100. I expected to get some replies, but I never did and I found that suspicious. The next thing I knew, the fellow that they sent out was writing up all kinds of clients in my area.

He was hijacking the responses that were coming in to the main office and instead of forwarding them to me, he was following up on them and collecting a full commission. At the same time, he was trying to convince me that it was his hard work that generated these new clients. If it smells like a rat, it's a friggin' rat! I quit the insurance gig as soon as my two-month wage expired.

I let the headquarters' manager know why, and I don't know if the other fellow ever got disciplined, but in my opinion he should have been fired. I am really not very fond of back stabbers and didn't want to work for a company that hires assholes like that.

A funny thing happened when I first applied. I met the headquarters' manager for an interview over supper, which he paid for. Of course I managed to tip my supper plate over the side of the table and catch most of it when it fell upside-down into my lap. I was thinking, Ahh crap, that should impress the hell out of him! So I said, "I guess I'm a little nervous." He was good about it so I don't think I lost too many brownie points.

Then he asked me if I was a procrastinator. I answered very quickly saying, "I don't even know what the word means." It impressed him that I was so much against procrastination that I would say that. Truth be told, I really did not know what that word meant! I do now though!

After my failed insurance agent attempt, I joined an institutional fire department. The Institutional Fire Department was a fire department located on the outskirts of our new city. There were seventeen firefighters employed there. I enjoyed ten years there before the government shut down that facility and I, along with everybody else in that institution was either laid off or placed in a different job in a different city.

However, during the years I worked on that fire dept. I never went to any structural fires, but I did go out on rescue calls. This institution was a multi acreage multi building facility with over 400 patients and an equal number of staff required to run everything. It was a government facility. One call was for a worker who was suffering from heat stroke and on the verge of passing out. He was barely coherent and laying on the roof of a grain silo. The roof was about 45 feet above the ground, right over a Holstein bull that was about 12 feet long and weighed about 4,000 pounds.

We put the aerial ladder in position and extended the ladder about four feet above where the guy was lying. I went up the ladder and struggled to get him onto the ladder with me. After about ten minutes I was successful in placing him under my arms in between the ladder and me.

Down below, my captain was looking up and watching the progress when my victim started to vomit. I yelled down to the captain, "This guy is puking so look out below or you're going to eat his lunch." Apparently they couldn't hear me because he was still looking up watching the progress when my victim started to vomit. I yelled down again, and they still couldn't hear me. They soon figured it out. I don't think they enjoyed the guy's lunch either!

On a boys' night out with fellow firefighters one evening, I went out with the guys to a cabaret in the downtown area underneath a pizza place in the basement. I was sitting around the table with a group of three other firefighters when a fellow in the bar sat on the arm of my chair. He turned to me and said, "I hope you don't mind me sharing your chair."

I said, "What do you think! You got your ass sticking in my face while I'm trying to have a drink. Of course I mind you sharing my chair." Then he got a little hostile and challenged me to go outside and duke it out. I told him to "fuck off". The bouncers got over to us quickly to prevent it from carrying on anymore. I drank for a couple of more hours, and when it was time to go home, I saw the guy sitting at a table closer to the door. I went over there and asked him if he still wanted to take it outside.

He had a few more drinks by then so he was a little braver and probably a little slower, but he came upstairs with me and we did a little tussling. He threw me into a large plate glass window on the building next door to the pizza place. Luckily it didn't break. I got up and he grabbed onto my arm again but when I pulled it away, he pulled the watch off my wrist and smashed it on the ground.

That's when the adrenaline kicked in. I kicked him and then hit him, and he fell to the ground with his hands on the cement. I stood on his fingers trapping both of his hands between my cowboy boots and the sidewalk. I told him he owed me $40 for my watch and that I wanted my money now. When I got off one of his hands, he reached into his pocket and pulled out his wallet to give me the $40 cash.

I was okay with that and the fight seemed to be over so I went home with my $40. I made a couple of bucks because I'm pretty sure I only paid $20 for that particular watch. I should have thanked him for replacing the old one.

While working at this institution, we firefighters often taught some of the mentally challenged patients how to ride bicycles. We had lots of spare time, and it was quite humorous watching them learn. Sometimes they would just go like hell straight into a wall, and other times they were successful in steering and stayed on the bicycle for longer periods of time.

One of the patients was named Donnie. He had a raspy voice and kind of a gangster appeal. We got along pretty good with him. One day the Minister of Health and his entourage came to inspect the institution. We told Donnie that he should go over to their car when they arrived and tell them to get the fuck out of here. We told him they didn't belong here, and he should let them know that.

This was all in humor (ours), of course, and Donnie did exactly as we told him to do. He rolled up beside the car on his bicycle and said, "Get the fuck out of here. We don't need you here, and we don't want you here! So fuck off and get out of here!"

With his raspy voice and his gangster demeanor, they took him fairly seriously, but they still got out of the car exercising caution and showing a little fear. We congratulated Donnie afterwards and he had a huge grin on his face because he had won our approval. Yeah, we were bad influences on those "kids". Everyone called them "kids", regardless of their age, due to their mental capacity but it was really a term of endearment.

While working there as a firefighter, again, I worked several different part time jobs, just as I had when I worked for the City Fire Department. One of these jobs was a guard at a Regional Correction Center. That's a job I wouldn't recommend to anyone.

I came to realize very quickly that many, not all, of the convicts in there are only there because they lack intelligence. Being a guard in a prison was like babysitting grown-ups. On my first day I was advised not to eat meals that were prepared by inmates. So basically, don't eat there unless you brought your own lunch.

I heard they spit and blew snot into your food. That's all I needed to hear. Lunch bag from home it was! I can still remember the words of my old police instructor saying, "The only difference between you and the guys behind bars right now, is that you bastards never got caught."

It appeared to me that there was a reason many of these inmates got caught. The average intellectual level seemed to be below par.

I didn't work there very long because I was working on a "call out" basis. They had a rule that if you were called out and refused work on three separate occasions, you were considered unreliable. I put that to the test and found it to be true. That was one of the tests I passed without having to study.

I was taken off the call-out list, but I netted some collectable uniform arm crests and still have one in my collection of badges from places I've worked. Since I only worked there for a couple of months and I was never told I was fired, I assumed I was just scratched off the list. If I was fired, it would have been the only time in my life I've ever been fired, but it would have been worth it.

I had another part-time job anyway working as an ambulance attendant. I found it a lot more interesting and satisfying. On that job I often did patient transfers. I once took a patient to a very remote community in a small aircraft. I was facing backwards because I had to keep an eye on my patient. That made me vulnerable to motion sickness.

The patient was a chatterbox and wouldn't shut up. I was getting close to vomiting, which was not something he needed on this flight. I finally had to tell him I couldn't talk to him anymore because if I did he was going to be wearing my breakfast. I'm sure he was now more concerned about my motion sickness than I was because he finally shut up. The airstrip there didn't even have a building let alone a bathroom. Instead they had wooden outhouses on the side of the runway where the planes landed. I quickly ran into one of those on arrival and barfed.

On the flight back I told the pilot I wanted him to land at the closest airport where I could catch a commercial flight so I could go home on a big plane. I was so sick that I was even willing to pay my own way. He talked me into staying when he said he'd let me fly the plane once airborne. His word was good, and I got to pull the wheel in and out a few times raising and lowering the altitude. I knew I wasn't really flying it, but it was still pretty cool to me. My motion sickness on the way home was negligible.

As a firefighter, I had plenty of days off to fill and there were times when I had political aspirations. I ran for the position of regional director of a large rural constituency. A regional director is a position equivalent to a mayor's position in larger centers but in the rural areas we called our elected leaders regional directors. I had plenty of days off to fill so why not give it a shot. I failed to win that position but I did win 75% of all the votes within my own community. However the candidate that I ran against was running for his second or third term and won 75% of the votes in the area that he lived in, which was a much larger area. That simply equates to 'I lost, he won." We moved to that rural area because we had a huge house built that was better suited to our family. It had 8 bedrooms and 3 bathrooms, a 5x10 pool table, 2 pin ball machines and a 'Pac man' video game table. I commuted 45 minutes each way on my work days to the Firehall.

My wife and I got involved in the community and joined the local community association. For years before we moved there, that association had been raising funds to build a community hall and they had enough to build one, but only if we did the work ourselves. So we did! However, without adequate fire protection, I convinced them to put a door on the front to house a fire truck. That way, the truck could be pulled outside when an event was held and I had a line on an old firetruck.

After we built the hall, I bought that old fire truck from a small city that had retired their 1942 "Bickle Seagrave" convertible fire pumper. It had a V-12 engine and came with a spare motor. I paid them $800 for all of it, and then our community raised the money to pay me back by having dances in the new fire hall. The only reason I was able to buy it so cheap was that the community I bought it from wanted to help us out because we did not have any support for a fire department from the Regional District. The reason I ran for and lost the Regional Director position was to gain that support.

I also sourced donations of fire protective gear from three different fire departments and got enough gear to outfit sixteen firefighters with fire resistant coats and uniform shirts. Some of the gear was borrowed from the Institution where I worked without their knowledge. It was redundant anyway. The land was public owned so no cost involved there either.

Now we had a fire hall and a fire truck. Over the years that followed after I left, it had the effect of putting tremendous pressure on the regional district because later-model equipment was required in order to qualify for Public Fire Protection Classification (a multi-national corporation that underwrites the bulk of all fire insurance claims). In order to achieve that approval, all fire departments had to have modern equipment. The main concern was that no fire fighting apparatus should be older than ten years. A 1942 fire pumper was most certainly not a modern piece of equipment!

It took a lot of posturing to convince residents that, with a fire hall, their home insurance policy would be cheaper, but only if they were situated within five miles of a fire hall and most of them were. My family and I moved out of that community when I was laid off from the fire department and diagnosed with cancer, (I'll elaborate on that in the next section), in order to downsize our financial commitments.

However, when we first moved into that area, they already had fire hydrants but no building. In order to fight fires they gathered a group of mostly senior citizens, both male and female, who agreed to attend fires. They planned to fight fires with hose that was in hose huts. The huts were strategically placed in a half a dozen locations around the community. The hose huts were designed to house wooden boxes of hose that slid off a platform onto a pick-up truck which would then be taken to a hydrant. This was not an ideal situation for firefighting. Once I was appointed Chief, I dismissed most of the older members of that volunteer brigade and recruited enough young men to form a 16 man fire department under my position of Chief.

It was easy to recruit them because I enticed them with beer and snacks at my place after practice. Some of them were bordering on being under 18 years of age but what the heck!

Here is a picture of the truck and some of my volunteer firefighters.

We hadn't had the fire truck in service for more than a month when we had a major fire. It was the first fire that any volunteers from our community had ever attended other than small grass fires.

The fire truck came in very handy that day and we were able to save a house that was attached to a large indoor swimming pool. We lost the pool building because it was fully involved when we arrived but we saved the house it was attached to as well as a 500 gallon propane tank piped in 5 feet from the burning building. Now, our volunteer fire department had experience!

Had we not purchased the old fire pumper, there would not have been any motivation to upgrade the equipment.

The constituents would not have benefitted from lower insurance rates and the community would have had to deal with fires using hose in hose huts for years to come.

I heard that the community eventually sold the 1942 fire

pumper to a small city fire department for a lot more than we paid for it. Now it is a parade truck, and it is still in that area today.

Part Eight:
Illness, Entrepreneurial Work, and Fun

BEFORE I START in on this section, I'll say up front that if I was reading what follows, I'd think this guy's life is almost over. Hell, pity aside, this cancer and PTSD stuff is just a little bump in my road through life. I'm writing down things in the order I remember them happening. I'm not looking for any pity. I love my life, good, bad and ugly, I own 'all of it'. Now to continue!

I believe the stress of being laid off after 13 years as a firefighter contributed to PTSD, possibly to cancer as well.

I was diagnosed with cancer at 35 years old. I had sixteen radiation treatments, followed by chemotherapy treatment I was allergic to. The radiation was applied to 100% of my body other than my eyeballs, which were covered with lead capsules. As a result, I lost all my hair, including eyebrows and nose hair.

I mention nose hair because I found it funny that when I lost those hairs, upon quick inhalation through my nose, my nostrils would stick together. I always wondered why in hell we had unsightly hairs sticking out of our nose. Now I know why. I also lost toenails and fingernails and could hardly walk because I was burned so badly.

Another interesting phenomena is that the toe and fingernails don't actually fall off. They just stop growing until the radiation discontinues. Once the radiation is no longer applied, they grow again, so I had a quarter-inch space between the new and the old-growth nails. Pretty interesting stuff I thought!

When I went for the radiation treatments, we didn't have much money so I qualified for free lodging at the cancer lodge located kitty corner from the cancer clinic. While staying at the cancer lodge, I was told that my treatments would result in weight loss. So I ate like a pig only to discover that, as usual, I did not conform to the rules and I gained weight. That was disappointing!

I thought it was hard times for me at the time, but after meeting a few of the other people staying at the cancer lodge, it made me realize that the position I was in was much better than what a lot of them were facing. I decided to give myself a "boot in the ass" and start thinking out a plan for the future. I bought a few books on auto body repair and painting. I had done some of this in the past, but I wanted to take it to the next level.

I went through a few bouts of depression with all that going on combined with the PTSD, (likely caused by what I've witnessed in life. I did leave out the most gruesome event I witnessed, for your sake!)

The cancers are part of life I learned to live with and I can control the PTSD more and more every year. I still cry sometimes when watching TV and something triggers it. My cancer treatments were effective enough that I'm still here at 73 years old! Cancer doesn't concern me much because they say only the good die young. My 'on going' cancers are slow growing and I'll likely die of old age rather than cancer so I'm just fine.

Soon after my dealings with disability, I applied for a couple of jobs to create a dependable cash flow, preferably something with pension plan. I applied for a position as a jail guard. I was still bald with no eyebrows from the radiation so I wore the wig the Cancer Agency gave me. That wig thoroughly undermined my self confidence and I botched the interview. Hell, I felt like I had a fur bearing animal on my head. All I could think of was "These guys think I brought my cat with me to this interview."

Now that the downside of my life is out there, lets get back to living large again.

Once we left that rural community and I was on the mend we entered into an agreement for sale on a house in which we negotiated extra funds to build a shop in the backyard. It was all a blessing in disguise. An agreement for sale means we purchased the place but would not be on the title until all financial commitments had been satisfied.

I had done quite a bit of construction in the past. That being said, when you do the work yourself, you can save at least 50% of the cost that you'd have to pay for somebody to do it for you. This particular house was in very rough shape, and we were going to have to do a lot of major construction to get things up to par. The basement floor had to be jack hammered up because it had huge cracks in it, and the foundation had to be bolstered up.

An "on site" shop was necessary to earn enough money to do the house repairs, so it was my first priority. I didn't bother to get a permit because they are a pain in the ass. I had my boys help me put the garage up on a long weekend when the building inspectors were not working. The shop was not very visible from the road, so I'm sure that to this day they don't even know that it's there.

I was proud of the fact that we were able to put up a garage and shingle the roof in one weekend. (I poured the pad previously). I did all the electrical and the gas line myself. My workmanship was apparently solid because nothing has fallen down or blown up since I built it.

I was operating an upholstery shop a few blocks away at the time because doing body work in my new shop would make too much of a mess to do upholstery. I learned to do upholstery when I was on the police department by hanging around "Ken's Upholstery." I chummed with Ken often and he was a great teacher. I bought my own machine in 1969, and I put it to work to bolster my income.

When I rented the shop for my upholstery. It included a fenced compound and the building was already partially rented by a couple of guys running a sandblasting business. We got along very well with one another and became good friends. I had a small car sales lot at that shop for some time as well but I only had a half-dozen cars there. The locked compound provided excellent security for their sandblasting equipment and for my cars.

There was a guard dog there that they had rescued from somewhere, and it was a pretty effective dog named Scruffy. He was a nasty little bastard. I tried to suck up to him by bringing him dog biscuits. He bit the hand that fed him. Mine! He bit me a couple of other times too. He would sneak up behind me when I was in the compound and bite me on the leg. If I turned to kick him when I saw him coming, he would not attack. He loved the element of surprise. It took some time before we became friends. I sure was glad when that day came.

With the shop going, I was now able to fix a car completely from upholstery, to engine, to bodywork. My skills in auto bodywork and engines were satisfactory, and with help from friends I managed to get through every issue on any car that had a problem.

I've been buying and selling cars and motorcycles since I was 18 years old and I kept a record; 159 cars, trucks, golf cars, tractors, excavator, bobcat, boats, quads and 13 trailers. Currently, I only have 6 of the above but I'm always looking for a good deal.

To land a good deal one should always look for the '3D' solution. The 3 'D's' are Divorce, Death and Destitution. These 'D's' almost always produce good investments. (If you can live with yourself). My view is 'To pass something up is to pass it to somebody else'. Snooze and you lose, so to speak. It's not a business, it's pocket money and better in my pocket than someone else's.

I have a funny story about buying a truck from the GM dealer that was located at the bottom of the hill from where we lived. I saw a really nice 1972 GMC 4 x 4 pick-up there.

It was a desirable truck so I went down and made an offer on it, but before I completed the purchase, I wanted the salesman to show me that the winch on the front of the truck was operational. The guy activated the switch from the inside of the cab without realizing the winch hook was hooked on to the front bumper. Unfortunately, once he flipped that switch, the winch started winding in the cable, it pulled the bumper down, making a big dent in it where the hook was docked.

It appeared that the salesman did not know how to operate the winch because he got out and looked for a knob that would allow the winch to freewheel so he could get the hook out of the bumper. He didn't see one, so he went in and got a set of keys for a GMC blazer that was parked on the lot. He also brought out a chain and hooked it to the back bumper of the blazer on one end and to the cable on the winch at the other end.

Now things were getting interesting! He told me to hold my foot on the brake. His plan was to drive the Blazer ahead and break the winch loose to force it into the freewheel position. He got into the Blazer and floored it while I held my foot on the brake of my truck to be. The back bumper came flying off the Blazer! This was getting really interesting now. A few of the other salesmen working there started to come out to watch the show. Finally, a mechanic came over and showed him how to operate the winch. I felt sorry for the guy, but he was in way over his head and had left his common sense at home that day.

The salesman also said that the truck just had the transmission rebuilt and other than the winch bumper, which he would replace, it was in excellent shape. I bought it. A few months down the road, the transmission went so I went back to the dealer and said, "Your salesman told me the transmission was just rebuilt. Can you tell me how a freshly rebuilt tranny can bag out so soon? To me it seems like either you got lied to by whoever traded it in, or your salesman lied because the transmission is toast. What can you do for me to rectify that?"

As I expected, the dealer denied culpability so I took the truck to a place called Tom's transmission, and he rebuilt it for me. He also wrote a thorough assessment of what he found in there for court purposes. I took that assessment and filed a claim through small claims court. The assessment indicated that there had never been any work done on that transmission before Tom's Transmission rebuilt it, and it also detailed how he knew that.

I won that case in small claims court. The dealer ended up paying me for what I had paid to fix the transmission. I have never minded going to court, and when you win in court, it is a great feeling.

Another time, my wife's brother came out to visit us and there wasn't enough booze in the house to satisfy our needs for the weekend so he drove me down to the local liquor store. We both went in and stocked up. When we were back in the car after we put the booze in the trunk, I got in the passenger side about the same time that a big

4 x 4 "jacked-up" truck pulled in to the angle parking spot on my side.

The prick that was driving the truck banged his door into my brother-in-law's mirror while getting out of his truck. My window was down so I said, "Hey, watch your goddamn door, you just hit the car."

His reply was, "Fuck you!"

That pissed me off, so I opened my door and bumped his door with it. That in turn had the effect of pissing him off, so he opened his truck door and whacked it into my brother-in-law's mirror again, only harder. I thought, Okay dude, the war is on!

My adrenaline was now activated and I cracked my door just slightly open, put my foot up against it, and then rocketed it into his door, making a huge dent in the side. After that he didn't appear to want to follow up anymore. (He must have seen the "crazy" in my eyes.) But he did say, "You better wait here because I'm going to phone the cops."

I said, "Fuck you!" and we left.

I don't know how the cops found us because my brother-in-law's car had plates on it from a different jurisdiction. However, this city wasn't that big a place so some cop car probably drove by my house and saw the red Oldsmobile sitting in my driveway. Before too long, a police officer came to my door and wanted to speak with me.

I invited him in but he chose to stay just inside the front door. I explained what had happened. The cop told me that both of us were being assholes about it, and we probably both deserved what we got. "However, the dent you put in his truck was far more severe than the damage I can see on your brother-in-law's car."

"That's not my fault," I said. "It wasn't for lack of him trying. It's just that his door kept hitting the mirror and that prevented any serious damage to the car door, but the mirror is chipped."

The cop said, "Well, that's hardly the same." Anyway, he was going to go back and tell the guy that I wanted to charge him because he wanted to charge me. "With any luck at all, he'll drop the charges and that will be it." The cop was right because the chip on Bob's door could easily be touched up with a dab of touch-up paint.

I never heard from him after that so I guess things went my way. I'd bet dollars to donuts though that the fellow learned to be a lot more careful when opening his door. Surely, my lesson on etiquette was something he will remember for life. As a rule, etiquette lessons are not something I offer but that day was different.

One time I was driving my truck home up a hill towards my house. My wife and oldest son were with me. My truck had a 454 big block so it had lots of jam, but I guess I wasn't going fast enough for the guy behind me. He was so close to my bumper that he got my attention. I flashed my brake lights at him a couple of times, but that just seemed to have the effect of drawing him in closer. My next move was to slow to a stop and let him pass. He simply stopped behind me and did not pass.

I got out of my truck and walked back to his driver side window and said, "Would you like me to open up the tailgate so you can just drive in, and I can take you the rest of the way home?" He just looked at me and didn't answer, so I got back in my truck and I floored it, spraying his car with gravel. That seemed to aggravate him a little bit because now it seemed that he might want to talk to me. He lost that chance though!

His driving was getting worse and his distance behind me was getting closer. I was close to my house, but I didn't want to pull into the driveway because then the guy would know where I lived. I went around the block and drove back down the hill. He followed me the whole time. Now I could have some fun!

I turned up a back road, which was mostly gravel and every few seconds I would spin the tires and spray him again with rocks. I figured that sooner or later he was going to get tired of this game and go back home.

It took a few more sprays before he finally gave up and turned off. My wife, my son, and I drove around a bit more to make sure that he couldn't see where we lived and then we went home. He had vanished. I parked my truck in the backyard behind the fence for a while. I think I gave a glass company some windshield replacement business. I'm all about supporting the local economy.

Around Christmas time, I would drive around the city, and if I saw an old truck, I would put a note on the windshield indicating that if the owner wanted to sell, I was willing to buy their truck for $200 or $300 (whichever price best fit the truck I was looking at). As a result, we normally had an average of six vehicles in our yard at all times. I would work on and complete them one at a time to get them ready to sell.

I turned back quite a few odometers when I was working on cars and trucks before it was illegal. (Well, maybe even a few after.) If the mileage was too high, lowering it was beneficial in a sale. When I was younger, I heard several guys say you could turn an odometer back by putting an electric drill on the cable and then spin it in reverse to reduce the miles.

Those guys didn't have a clue. I tried it with a washing machine motor on a car I was selling because I wanted to turn off a lot of miles. I had that washing machine motor spinning backwards for over 24 hours, and it didn't even turn back 10,000 miles on the car.

So in order to turn them back thousands of miles, I had to pull out the gauge cluster and disconnect bulbs and clips after disconnecting the speedometer cable.[1] That gave me access to the odometer roll. I could pull the roll of numbers right out to see what kept the numbers in a straight line. It was a very thin plastic spacer that held upright notches in place so the numbers didn't all spin at the same time.

You had to be very careful when pulling off that plastic spacer because it was brittle and made to break. I had to be very patient and pull it off ever so slowly and then re-apply it the same way when I was satisfied with the numbers that were showing. The car sales lots were doing it too. Hell, one odometer on a 63 Chev hard-top even

---

[1] The newer cars no longer have speedometer cables and the workings are generally electronic, but back then the deception was fairly easy. With newer cars, you need to find an instrument cluster at an auto wrecker with lower miles. Then it's a simple switch.

had a note on the back of the instrument cluster that said, "What are you doing back here. It's already been turned back once."

I also started a small steam cleaning business to steam engines and equipment for customers. And in addition to that, I bought some insulation blowing machines that I placed in a few building supply businesses so that they could rent them out to the customers who bought cellulose insulation from them. I took in a few jobs adding insulation to houses that were already built but were under insulated. This generated more income from my insulation blowing machines.

However, that proved to be a mistake because there was always a mess when I had the attic entry door open. When you cause dust to cover every piece of furniture in someone's house, they tend to get a tad irate. Rather than deal with hostility, I sold the machines. The building supply places that were supposed to be renting them out were not reporting when they were rented out and were ripping me off anyway, so selling them was the right decision.

Another thing I did was to go into the video arcade, video poker, and jukebox business, and I negotiated machine placement in a few bars here and there. However, it was a cutthroat business. Competitors would stick pins in the speaker wires of their competition or jam up the coin mechanisms. I lost money on down time when the machines malfunctioned. When they needed repair, I had to drive hundreds of miles to the closest place that repaired and serviced them.

One time, I took my fourteen-year-old son with me to the repair facility but going back home the same day had too many risks. I went to get a hotel for the night, but the hotel clerk I was dealing with must have thought I was some kind of a pervert who was checking in with a young boy to have sex with.

Why did I think that? Because when we went to the room and pulled back the covers on the bed there were pubic hairs all over the pillowslips. I figured this room was used for hookers and johns. I was pissed right off, mostly because this clerk had pegged me for a pervert. I should have clued in that this place was a dump because the clerk was behind a cage of metal bars at the front counter. I was looking for the cheapest accommodation, not the safest one. I went back to see the clerk right away and expressed my concerns. I'm sure had the look of a murderous felon on my face when I demanded my money back. He knew he used poor judgment and my money was refunded.

Then, I decided to risk the drive home that night. After driving for only a short while, I was very concerned that I would fall asleep. I thought about how devastated my wife would be if I were to crash and if our son and I were killed. If it was just me who was killed, not so much! Why? Because we hunted together until we realized we both had life insurance policies, so neither of us wanted to walk in front of the other.

Then I thought of the solution. My son did not have a driver's license or a learner's permit, but he drove his motorcycle a lot on back roads so he had a sense of the rules of the road. If I got him to drive, he would be extremely excited – so much so, that he wouldn't be able to sleep even if he was tired.

My son only had to wake me up once to ask me how to get through a city. He did a great job, and I got plenty of sleep so we made it home safely. I had to take a barrage of angry criticism from my wife. When she is mad, she uses a lot of profane words, let me tell you! But I figured all's well that ends well.

Then there was my "money laundering" days! I bought and sold a lot of stuff. When a good deal comes up, you need to be first and fast to scoop the deal. For that reason, I always kept about $5,000 at the house in case the bank was closed. It also enabled me to go straight to the seller, hopefully before someone else. However, it worried me to have that much cash in the house. My solution was to hide it well so nobody could find it. So I jack hammered a hole in the basement floor under the stairs. I cemented a small safe in the hole. I made a nice edge on it, then put a nice fitting wooden lid over it all, and stenciled it "water shut off". My money was safe in there now. All I had to do was wait a few days until the cement hardened.

The safe had a combination lock on a round door, so I cemented it in completely leaving only that round door exposed. Three days later, I went down to check if the cement was hard and everything was copasetic. Yup, I had done a good job, so I spun the numbers to open the small round door, and it wouldn't open. Why it wouldn't open is because the lid was part of the round combination door and I cemented it in because it looked like it was a separate door. It wasn't! Ahh shit! My money was in there! So

I chiseled, hammered, and drilled until the combination mechanism was gone, and I had access to the safe. Then, I welded on a tin lid with a hinge and put a hasp on it with a padlock. The wooden water shut off lid still fit over it perfectly and looked genuine. My money was safe!

A couple of weeks later I went in to get some money out and guess what? The safe was no longer air proof so moisture had gotten in and my money was all moldy! My wife and I spent hours washing it and then laying out bills of almost every denomination on our king-sized bed. Every inch of the bed was covered. If that's not money laundering, I don't know what you would call it.

I bought a 14-foot boat with a 50-horse motor on it really cheap. It needed an awful lot of work. I put a new windshield on it, painted it, painted the engine, detailed everything, and reupholstered the seats. It looked pretty damn good. We phoned a couple that lived a few blocks away and told them we were about to take our new boat out on its maiden voyage. It wasn't quite dark yet, so they said they would love to come. We met them down at the boat launch, put the boat in the lake, and away we went. The men sat in the front on top of the seat backs; the ladies sat in the back with their feet on the floor. Of course we brought beer!

We stopped way out in the lake to drink a few beers. Before too long, our wives complained their feet were getting wet. Shit! I forgot to put the drain plug back in the hole. That was a simple fix. It was a very big lake, and we were quite far from our boat launch, so we started back.

When you are moving at a good speed, the water goes back out the drain hole, so when it was no longer an issue, the girls put the plug back in. Then we faced another problem. It was dark and we couldn't see exactly where our boat launch was. To compound that, it started to rain. Then we started to get thunder and lightning. Now we were in trouble. The last place you want to be in a lightning storm is in the middle of a lake.

It also appeared that we were lost. I'd had enough to drink that it didn't concern me, and I said in a drunken slur, "I'ff neffer been loshed before. I jus' been confoozed a bit, neffer loshed!" My passengers were giving me conflicting guidance so I just told them to shut up, "Cuz I got thish!" I just followed the shoreline until we were in familiar territory.

We were lucky and made it back without dying. We quickly loaded the boat on the trailer and drove home. There was a short cut home, but it was a rough uphill road that only a 4 x 4 could go up, especially in the rain. Lucky us! We were in a 4 x 4, so we took the short cut. I'd had enough to drink so that nothing daunted me, and we went up at a pretty good speed.

The boat fell off the trailer because I forgot to anchor the stern to the trailer. Even worse, I didn't even notice when it fell off. Worse yet, it fell off the side of the trailer upside down because the bow was the only part tied to the trailer. I was dragging the boat upside-down beside the trailer. I shaved off the windshield, the top of the motor cover, and the top of the seats, and I broke off the lights and scratched the body. Damn! When I looked down the hill it looked like a bomb had gone off. Broken windshield pieces, life jackets, beer bottles, boat parts, oars, etc. They were spread all over hell, which was exactly what my wife was giving me. After gathering up all the usable shrapnel, I parked it in the garage so I could work on it to fix my mistakes and keep me away from the wife for a few days.

Another summer, I went to a golf tournament with a friend and a few buddies. We all planned on meeting at the golf course in a town about two hours away. Rick and I went in my motorhome, so we didn't have to rent a motel. As expected, there was an over abundance of liquor involved and both Rick and I were still shit-faced drunk in the morning. When we woke up and looked out the window, we couldn't even tell where we were. It was in a nice place though, lots of greenery and trees, and it was also nice and quiet. However, we still had no idea where we were, so we got out and had a look around.

Oh shit! We were parked at the golf course. Worse yet, we were parked on the first hole on the grass right between the tee-off markers. Thank God, it was early enough that there was no one working at the golf course yet. I quickly moved the motorhome into the parking lot. Dodged that bullet but more to come!

We hadn't sobered up enough to start drinking again, but that didn't stop us. We kept knocking back those beers. That put me into another drunken stupor for pretty much the rest of the day. However, I still joined in on the golf. I couldn't even hit the ball with my club unless I swung at it enough times that I finally got lucky. I even fell down a few times when swinging the club.

Long story short, I only made one great shot. It was on the eighteenth hole right in front of the clubhouse. The balcony was full of people, most of whom I knew. I was about 100 yards from the pin, and after a few swings at the ball, I hit it and it went right into the cup.

There were dozens of guys watching, and they gave me a well-deserved round of applause. To show my gratitude, I turned around and pulled down my pants enough to show them a big flesh-colored moon. That created another round of applause.

Then when I got up to the green, I was surprised to see there were quite a few women on the balcony, not just men. So I didn't join in for refreshments after the game. Instead, I did something really stupid. I drove straight home. I don't know how I made it home, but I did. People were looking for me but I was nowhere to be found.

Rick had to get a ride back with someone else, and the next day I was given a play–by-play from my buddies of all the stupid stuff I had pulled off that weekend. My pants were the last thing I pulled off. That brings us to the "end" of this story.

One day, my wife questioned me as to why I had so many irons in the fire. There were times when she didn't know which uniform to have ready when I arrived home. There were uniforms from the fire department, the ambulance, and the correction facility. I gave her a short answer, "SIX KIDS!"

I've owned three cube vans over the years. With the cube van and a trailer, we would regularly go to an auction sale in a neighboring town that was about an hour and a half away. We would bid on items that we could get dirt-cheap. Even with paying the sales tax and the auctioneer's 15% fee, we were able to make pretty good money just by taking the stuff we bought there to an auction in the city where we lived. The selling auctioneer added a fee to re-sell the stuff too, but we still made a good profit.

It was hard to believe that what we generally paid in the smaller town was so much less than what people would pay in a bigger city for the same merchandise. It was unusual but it was a fact. My good friend who lived in the place with the cheaper auction also added to the cost by humoring himself when sitting behind me and bidding me up. I caught him when I heard him and his brother-in-law giggling when I was bidding. After I caught the buggers, I made sure I sat behind them at the auctions because they were getting to be expensive friends.

Another friend of mine bought a disco that was three and a half hours away in a bigger center. It was set up for teenagers to come and spend money on fries and drinks and to meet and dance. Apparently it wasn't a very good business so they sold the building to my friend.

He was eager to start a bingo hall in that facility, but the people he bought it from still hadn't cleared it out. There were all kinds of tables, bar chairs, a pool table, dance floor, cooler doors, glasses, and even a 20-foot pink awning. My friend asked me if I would be interested in taking everything out of there, and then I could keep it all at no cost to me. My wages would be what I could sell all the stuff for.

I agreed to do it, so I took a couple of my boys there and rented a large storage unit nearby. We hauled all that stuff with my cube van to the storage place then took one load back home with us that day. The rest of it, I planned on picking up at a later date. However, about a week later my friend phoned me again and said that the previous owner contacted him wanting to get his stuff back! Too late! There was no legal obligation for him to give the guy his stuff back.

My friend gave him my number and the guy called me. I told him that if he were willing to pay wages for me and my helpers and my storage fees, gas, and expenses, I would deliver the stuff that I had taken. He agreed and said that he'd have a check for me when I get there. He didn't bother asking me for an amount, and I hadn't given him a price. He gave me the impression he was blowing smoke out of his ass so I didn't bother taking the stuff back.

A week later, the guy phoned me again and said, "Where is my stuff?"

I said, "I delivered it last week but you weren't there, so I dropped it off in the alley behind the building. When do I get the check that you promised me?"

If he had been legitimate, he would have asked me for an amount on the first phone call. Let's face it; he had no intention of paying me anything. He did, however, tell me to go fuck myself. Fair enough, I could live with that! I never heard from him after that.

I waited a few weeks before going to get the rest of the stuff out of that storage unit. I had my cube van loaded down with a heavy-duty trailer in tow. I put the 20-foot pink awning on the top of the van and tied it down. In the trailer I was towing, I had all of the heavy two-by-six boards that supported the hardwood dance floor plus all the hardwood and several tables and chairs. Those two-by-six boards were twelve feet long and my trailer was only eight, so they extended out the back of the trailer by four feet.

It's never good when you have more than half the weight behind the axles on a trailer because when you try to drive at high speeds, the trailer starts to sway back and forth, which eventually can cause you to lose control of the vehicle. In order to get more weight over the front part of the trailer, I stopped at every temporary traffic sign on the side of the road that had sandbags on it and I borrowed them to put on the A-frame of the trailer at the front. That put more weight in front of the axle than behind.

That worked a bit and enabled me to go slightly faster, but I still had to stay close to the posted speed. If there had been more temporary signs, I could have solved the problem completely, but you can only work with what's available.

Now my only concern was going by the weigh scales with what looked like a circus wagon: a white cube van pulling a trailer with twenty twelve-foot, two–by-six boards hanging out the back. I also had a pink quarter round awning twenty feet long and four feet in diameter on top of the roof. To top it off, the stolen sandbags were on the front "A" frame of the trailer. It just would not have gone over very well at the weigh scales.

My strategy was to wait until I saw a bus approaching from behind and then try to get the bus to shield my vehicle from the sight of the people working at the weigh scale. It almost worked except I couldn't quite keep up to the speed of the bus without the trailer starting to sway again. By the time I got up to the weigh scale, I was about half visible and the bus was still pulling away from me.

However, my timing was perfect. The bus served as a "blind" for the pink awning and only the trailer was visible from the scales. I assumed the officials working at the weigh scale were too busy to notice, but in any event it was my lucky day and I made it all the way home with my load. I had no trouble selling the two-by-sixes or the hardwood flooring, and I got rid of a lot of other stuff by using Kijiji. However, the pink awning did not get any response and I had advertised it for only $150.

As a result I took that pink awning to the auction, and they sold it for $700. Holy shit! What a shock! That was a huge surprise and a very nice profit for me even after paying them their commission. They also auctioned off the rest of the items that I was unable to sell through Kijiji, and it was a good day for the pocketbook, even after paying my boys for their help.

While I was at an auction, I bid on a small trailer with antique wooden spoke wheels on it. I only paid $50 for it, and I figured I could sell the wheels for a couple hundred bucks and the trailer for $150. There was a car engine in the back of the trailer, and at the end of the auction, the person who bought the car engine asked me if he could use my trailer to take his engine home.

I said, "I'll do you one better. I paid $50 plus fees and tax for the trailer, so you give me $100 and you can take it home with your engine." I was being extremely generous and thought a small profit for absolutely no work was profit enough.

The guy said, "No way. I don't need a trailer." So I got pissed off and said, "Take your damn engine off then so I can take my trailer home." Then I towed my trailer back home an hour and a half away with no license plate on it. I later sold it for $200 after I had taken off the wheels and put on regular rims. I sold the wheels for another $100. I was sure glad the guy didn't buy it for the price I had offered to him.

The buddy at the auction who was bidding me up was a very close and dear friend. He has taught me an awful lot over the years. His sense of humor is a bit off the wall (I think mine is too), and he is quite laid back. If you're not paying attention, he can make you feel pretty silly very quickly.

I remember one day our family was traveling out to his house to visit, and I was running late. I have a tendency to freak out when I can't make it someplace on time, and I was in that state on the way to his place. There was a rodeo happening in a small town between his place and mine. When I got to that town, there was so much traffic that it put me into a deeper state of stress. I was following traffic at about five mph or less thinking, "I'm going to be so late!"

The next thing I know when I looked to the right, I saw my buddy casually leaning up against the fence alongside his family. I pulled off the road, drove up to him, and said, "What are you doing here? I'm rushing like hell to get to your place, and you're slumming here." He calmly said, "Why hurry? I'm not even home." He looked at me confused as to why I'd be in such a state of panic.

Another time, I was out hunting with him and I saw a bear on the hillside beside the road. I was riding with him so I asked him to pull over. I got out of the car and took aim at the bear. Once again, he calmly said, "Don't shoot him."

I shot anyway because I was never one to listen. I then said, "Why not?" He said, "Because he's on a hill so he'll roll down here, and if you didn't kill him, he will probably kill you."

He was correct. The bear did roll down the hill all the way to my feet. When I saw the bear rolling down towards me, all I could think of was, "Shit! I'm going to die now!" I was lucky the shot was a kill shot but things could've been a whole lot different.

My wife and I, with our six kids, used to go on holiday camping trips with him and his wife and their kids and their sister, brother, and his child. Those were some of the best vacations we have ever been on. Our kids were all age compatible. Our combined families, seventeen in total, drew an awful lot of attention. We'd set up tables at the side of the road or in parking lots. Foldable tables with umbrellas and seventeen people picnicking in odd places was a rare sight. We enjoyed the comments people made about it. Often we had several strangers and passers by stop and ask what it was we were selling. With eleven kids running around I was surprised they had to ask. I replied, "Want to buy a kid? We have a good selection!"

I remember one time I had just arrived at my friend's place and we sat down for a coffee when one of his friends came running in through the back door and said, "There's a moose up on the hill."

He immediately jumped into action, grabbed a couple of rifles, gave one to me, and then he and his wife and I drove up to where the individual said the moose was last seen. They dropped me off and then drove further down the road. The plan was to walk towards each other in hopes of containing the moose between us so that one of us was able to shoot it.

I was walking along a wildlife trail for about ten minutes looking for the moose but the only thought that was going through my head was, "Damn! I'm wearing a brown leather jacket but through the trees it's possible that I might be mistaken for the moose." I was pretty sure that my buddy would never fire unless he knew exactly what he was aiming at, but what about others out hunting? I got the hell off the game trail. The moose got away.

As a final insert to this section which encompasses fun, I'll mention my driving habits. They are bad. Why? Because I'm an adrenaline junkie. I've wrecked a lot of cars and motorcycles. Here are a couple of examples.

I have been pretty good about avoiding speeding tickets. In my 40's, I was with my wife and my dad. We were all coming back from a family visit hundreds of miles away. Just before we were half way home, a guy passed me and I was already going about twenty over the limit. I stayed right with him and his speed was picking up.

Then, all of a sudden, an oncoming cop car turned on his lights and pulled to the right. When the traffic cleared I saw him through my rear view mirror making a U-turn. Oh-oh, I thought to myself, "If I'm the first car he catches up to, the guy in the other car gets away, so I've got to get in front of the other guy."

It looked like the other guy was ready to surrender because he slowed down and was waiting for the cop to catch up. I flew past him and continued on at a high rate of speed pulling further and further away from him until I couldn't see him any more,

My dad and wife were in panic mode yelling at me, but I ignored them. I was too busy thinking. I came upon a restaurant so I pulled in behind it right off the highway and out of sight.

They both asked, "What are you doing?"

I said, "I'm going in for a coffee until all this clears itself up." They both followed me in with looks of confusion on their faces. After about a half an hour we were on our way again and never saw the cop anywhere. I had avoided another ticket.

Another time, my wife and I were highway driving to somewhere far away and traffic was slow, so I started to pass groups of cars at a time, whenever there was an opportunity.

I was driving at a high rate of speed in the oncoming lane, when a guy pulled out of the slow traffic a few cars ahead, so I tailgated him. We were both way over the speed limit in the oncoming lane when we blew by a cop in the slow lane. "Shit!" I looked in my rear-view mirror and, yup, he pulled out after us. As soon as I saw the cop, I slowed right down and pulled back into the slow lane behind some other cars. The cop blew by me to chase the guy I had been tailgating and I was pretty damn sure once he pulled that guy over, he was going to wait for me and pull me over as well.

No way I was going to let that happen. I slowed down and let all the traffic by. Then when it was clear, I did a U-turn and we went back to the last city I passed, some ten miles back. We took an hour-long lunch break and then got back on track. We never saw the cop after that. I think I'm getting pretty darn good at "fooling the fuzz".

Part Nine:
Border Services Officer on the 'Coast'

AFTER A TWO year stint of self employment and feast or famine income, I saw an ad in the paper where the federal government was looking to hire border guards so I applied for it and got an interview. One of the requirements was a minimum of a high-school education. I didn't even complete grade ten. Not a problem! I included my wife's certificate of graduation and accompanying documents showing her grades. She did well, so all I had to do was forge my name on a copy of her proof of education and submit that as my proof of education. It worked well because I was eventually hired. However, my Application had been on file for almost six months. At the time I applied I was told that the application would only be on file for six months so I phoned them and asked if there were any openings because I was really interested in the job and hadn't heard anything. I don't know who I was talking to when I phoned but the guy chuckled and said, "If you would like to have a job right away you can have it, but you'd have to work on the Pacific Coast. Ha! Ha!" That surprised me but I have never been one to have to think about things very long so I answered right away. I said, "Sure I'll work there."

That surprised him but he said they would be getting in touch with me shortly. They did and offered me a job at the Pacific Coast. When they called, they asked me when I would be able to start. It was a Friday and I asked him when they would like me there. He jokingly said, "How about Monday?" I said, "That would be great." They told me where to report and to whom. My wife was out grocery shopping when I got the good news that I had landed a job.

When she returned, I told her we were moving. She was flabbergasted! You just built a shop, we just totally renovated this house, you have an upholstery shop, you have a half a dozen vehicles in the yard that need finishing.

What the hell is wrong with you! Furthermore, we still have two kids at home. What now? I told her I started in two days. I think she wanted to kill me and that interfered with my packing for the coast.

Before we were able to buy a house on the coast, I rented an apartment there for six months. We had to wait before we could qualify to buy a house because my position with border services was as a term employee. I needed to be a permanent employee in order to get a mortgage.

Of course, the organization is better off financially with more employees in term positions because there are not as many paid benefits for them to cover. Enough was enough. After 6 months of driving 3 hours back and forth to finish cars and tying up loose ends, I asked for an audience with the local chief and explained my family situation to him. At that time, I indicated I had no other option than to submit my resignation and move on to a more stable employment opportunity. Fortunately, he understood and activated my permanent position.

My wonderful wife finished off the body work on the vehicles in the yard and I came home every weekend to paint them and help her out packing up and selling stuff.

I sold the house to a friend who didn't have a down payment. We faked one though so he could get a mortgage. I paid off the agreement for sale and we bought a house on the coast.

Funny thing though. While renting the apartment, it was unfurnished and I slept on a four-inch foam mattress on the floor. In the first week, I realized that the previous tenant had a cat because when I was reading one night with the lamp on, it attracted fleas. My first few weeks at work were in a classroom, and while sitting around a table with my classmates, the lady sitting beside me looked at me in horror when a flea jumped off my sleeve and landed on the table between us. I looked at her and shrugged it off with a sheepish grin. Obviously it didn't leave a good impression even though I explained the reason for it. My landlord at the apartment eventually sprayed the apartment. For a couple of days, I lived in that poisonous atmosphere, but the flea problem was solved.

After my initial training I went right to work as a rookie border officer and had a handgun seizure on my first day.

In fact my enforcement record was above normal. I caught a lot of smugglers, many with drugs and also some very high value enforcement actions. 'Birds of a feather', you might suspect?

I learned a few different interview techniques on my four years on the police department and improved upon them in my twenty years as a federal border officer. When working at the border I was very successful in gleaning the truth within a few minutes. I would let people sweat while waiting so that they would overthink their predicament. For instance, when interviewing a couple, I know they knew they were in trouble and were well aware I would eventually ask questions to which they both won't give the same answer.

At some point they will just want to get it over with badly enough that they would tell the truth. When lying to officials, people are stressed. Once they tell all, they feel a tremendous sense of relief, and it's noticeable. It's quite comical, and to me, it was a game that I played better than they did.

Very early in my career, I dealt with an elderly lady whom I could never forget. I laugh about the experience to this day. She was sent in from primary for a secondary examination and the card issued at primary was coded to reflect verification of her declaration of "no alcohol purchased". I've never been one to get too concerned about smuggled alcohol because I was a federal employee and tax on alcohol is not really a federal issue. This particular elderly lady was smuggling a bottle in such a conspicuous way that I found it humorous. She had a large bottle stuffed in to a small purse that she set on the counter right in front of me. Even before going out to check her car (which I did afterward), I asked her what was in the purse.

She said, "Private and personal use ladies' items." Okay! That momentarily stumped me so I said, "I'm going to have to inspect your purse." She objected so I said, "I'll be right back with a female officer who will be checking your purse."

I left her for less than a minute and when I returned with a female officer the purse was no longer bulging, indicating that whatever she had in there had been removed. In addition, it was obvious that she had first attempted to hide the bottle in the front of her pants because her zipper and clasp were now broken exposing her underwear.

I damn near burst out laughing but retained my composure and said, "Hiding a bottle in your pants didn't work out so well I see," and I pointed to her now undone pants. "What did you do with the bottle that was in the purse?" I walked around the counter expecting it to be on the floor at her feet but it wasn't.

I walked out the nearby door and recovered a 26-ounce bottle of vodka that had carefully been placed against the wall just outside the door. The female officer with me inspected her purse and no feminine products were found. My, my, what a surprise! I picked up the bottle and put it in the evidence room as a lost and found item. After checking her car I released her. The female officer and I were both chuckling about the whole situation. It was extremely unusual, very comical, and it made my day. I wish she was my grandmother!

I avoided chicken-shit seizure actions like undeclared leather jackets or a bottle of booze, but I was the primary point officer on what was the largest cocaine seizure in the history of the West Coast ports at that time. It was 26 kilograms of cocaine. The cocaine came in a false compartment under the trunk flooring of a vehicle. The license number is all we had to go on, and the information was provided on a typed sheet with dozens of license plates numbers on it. Computers were not used back then, and there were no electronic license plate readers either, so I made a habit of checking every plate against that sheet. Many of the officers did not.

This particular vehicle sported a license plate that was on that list as a "watch for" with regards to drug smuggling. There was a young lady driving and she was the sole occupant. I handed her a referral card, but I didn't want to alert her as to why I was sending her in for a secondary examination. So to avoid making her suspicious, I said, "I just want someone to verify that you have no undeclared purchases in your vehicle." That way she would not have caught on that she was being sent over to be searched for drugs that I suspected she might be smuggling. "I coded the card for drugs."

To tell her it was to verify she didn't have any undeclared goods turned out to be a mistake because she must have repeated that to the female customs inspector who came out to examine her car. The inspector looked in the trunk, closed the trunk, and basically didn't look at anything. That inspector didn't even notice the code number I wrote on the card was for "drugs" not merchandise. I was going crazy watching from my booth, so I phoned in to my supervisor and said, "I sent a referral in and coded the card for a drug referral. Lorna is out there right now and is about to release her. She never looked at a fucking thing." It pissed me off because she was too lazy to do a good job, let alone look at the damn card to check for the coding.

I was angry! The referral had come from a reliable source, so it was worth a good look, and it didn't get one. He ran out to the car just as Lorna was walking away, and 'he' further detained the female occupant. That supervisor took over the secondary examination and within a few minutes was pulling kilo after kilo of cocaine out of the trunk. I was happy to see that the referral was successful. However it shocked me to see the kilos of cocaine being stacked on the sidewalk alongside the building. That was half a million dollars worth of cocaine placed in plain view of the public. Think about that! We weren't even armed then!

Often after working a three to eleven p.m. shift, as many as six or eight of us would go to a bar on the other side of the border and have a few drinks to wind down from the days' activities. What was unusual about that was that none of us changed out of our uniforms. At that time, our uniforms were a very bright color and very noticeable to all of the patrons in the bar, especially because of the agency identification badges on the upper arms.

So we simply turned our uniform jackets inside out. It looked ridiculous and probably attracted a hell of a lot more attention that way because all the inner padding was showing, making it perfectly obvious the jackets were inside out. To top it off, the inner padding was sewn in and protruded up around the shoulders and sported shiny, bright silk-looking material while the rest of the inside view was the same color as the outside of the jacket. We were boisterous and not well behaved, which would have attracted even more attention. Then when the bar closed most of us drove home while over the legal limit. Those were the days!

Party time in my motorhome after work happened occasionally as well. Half a dozen of us would pile in and drive past our port office. But before we did, I stopped at the duty-free store and each of us bought a bottle of hard liquor or beer or wine. Then we'd drive into "no man's land" and park there to drink and bullshit until our booze was gone. When I say "no man's land" I refer to the space between the two countries. The space starts once passing the border office of one country but not yet reaching the border office of the other. Technically we hadn't left our country yet because the hard border was marked by metal posts. We hadn't crossed the markers, so we hadn't entered the next country.

There was a small parking area adjacent to a turn-around lane that I used when it was time to return home once I woke up sober. I never had to lie to any of my co-workers when asked how long I'd been out of the country. I also never had to lie when I was asked if I brought back anything back. I could answer in good conscience, "No, I am not bringing anything back, and I never left the country because I pulled over and slept in the parking area without actually leaving." I had empties in my garbage but empties are not taxable.

Sometimes one or two other border officers spent the night in no man's land as well so they didn't have to drive home after drinking, but their declarations were the same as mine. In a way it was cheating the system, but what are systems for if you can't cheat them every once in a while!

I'm not saying I wouldn't or didn't ever smuggle anything back. Of course I did! Especially after we moved inland to a smaller Port Office. Hell, I renovated my house there before I retired and brought back truckloads of undeclared goods. Do you think that aging would make me an angel?

As a point of interest, I'm going to mention that if and when you ever have to deal with customs, do so remembering that you do not have power over people in a uniform. You may think you are getting the last word but that is not necessarily the case. I will give you an example. A commercial truck driver came into the port because he was referred for a secondary examination. A secondary examination involves someone going out and having a good thorough look through the cab, the trailer, under the trailer, etc.

I went out to the truck with the owner operator at my side, and as I was about to get in, he told me not to go in there with my boots on. "Okay," I said, while thinking, "Oh, oh! I have an asshole here." I said, "In that case, when you're ready to let me look in your truck let me know, and I'll come back out, but I won't be taking off my boots. Until then, you are not permitted to leave, and you will stay here until someone has examined the vehicle inside and out. Do you understand me?" He cussed at me and gave me a threatening look. However he seemed to get the idea very quickly and gave me permission to search.

I didn't want him looking over my shoulder while I was looking through his truck so I told him to go into the office, sit down, and wait until I was finished. Keep in mind that when you get somebody with attitude, they tend to stand outside and give you a play-by-play of what you're looking at. I don't need a play-by-play when I'm looking at something.

Now that he had pissed me off, I felt the need to exercise a little pay back. So while I was looking through the cab I found his shaving kit and removed his toothbrush from the kit. Then I cleaned off the bottom of my boot with it before placing it back. That satisfied my vindictive and evil mind. Never underestimate the potential of a person in uniform when you piss them off. They just might have an ugly side.

This next story is about something that happened at a commercial crossing on the Coast. It is a troubling story to say the least. That particular border crossing is one of the main crossings for commercial goods being delivered by transport trucks. At that time the trucks had their own two lanes to enter the country. Those lanes were situated on the opposite side of the building from where the car traffic clears customs.

Back in those days, truckers did not usually have proper manifests with them to accompany their load, so they parked in a compound and walked across the street to a customs broker who would process a manifest. Then the driver would take his paperwork into the commercial customs clearance office to be processed. Sometimes the brokers were so busy the truckers had to wait to get their papers. One driver was told that processing his paperwork would be at least an hour so he went back to where his truck was parked. For some reason he sat down on the pavement and propped his back up against the rear wheel of the trailer parked next to him.

The driver of the truck whose trailer he propped up against, had no idea the guy was there. He left, and when the truck rolled forward, the sleeping trucker rolled with it until his head was pinned under the wheel where it was crushed by 40,000 pounds of weight. The head was almost gone except for bone, blood, and hair. Death would have been instant. The truck responsible left without the driver ever knowing he had just crushed someone's head, and he/she was never identified. The scene was extremely gruesome.

I do not like federal traffic cops! One time when I was allegedly speeding along one road and turned right on to another, I was pulled over by a federal officer. I had driven along that road for at least a half mile before he stopped me and gave me a ticket. He not only ticketed me for speeding, but he also gave me another one for $75 for failing to produce my driver's license which I had left in my other pants. I was still in uniform so that angered me, and I called him a "fucking Dillinger bastard". Then we parted ways.

After looking the speeding ticket over I realized that he had made an error on either the date or the location, but I can't remember which. So I went into the courthouse and had the ticket quashed because of the error. Once this "boy scout" had been notified that the entire ticket was quashed, he took issue. He re-issued the speeding ticket with the correct information. Getting the tickets quashed really pissed off this arrogant cop. How dare I correct his near perfect work? Calling him a "Dillinger bastard" when he wrote the tickets probably hurt his tender feelings too. Either that or he just enjoyed being a dick-head. I suspected the latter.

I was out of town the day that cop delivered a new summons to my house and my son answered the door. My son phoned me immediately and told me the cop had just delivered a re-issued speeding ticket. He told me the cop car was still in the driveway, and he was writing notes. I told my son to go out and tell the cop to get the fuck off my property. That should yank his chain a bit! He did leave when my son told him to, so I chalked that one up as a win.

Then I pleaded "not guilty" in court, and in giving my evidence said, "Your honor, this ticket was originally quashed because this officer (not good to call him a dickhead in court) made an error on it, and now he's doing it again. I believe he wrote the wrong road on the original ticket as well. I wasn't even on the road that was written on the ticket."

The judge gave me the benefit of doubt and ruled in my favor, telling the policeman that I was a customs officer and therefore not likely to lie in court. Hahahahaha! The cop was so angered that he went to speak to my chief at the crossing where I worked and complained to him that I lied in court to avoid a speeding ticket that he had issued. My chief said to him, "Look, you had your day in court, so let it go." I never heard from that cop again. My chief told me about the cop's visit, and I was very happy to hear he stood up for me. He probably didn't like traffic cops either.

Two years after entering into my customs career, I had a pretty high enforcement record, particularly in relation to firearms and drug seizures. Someone in the "interdiction and intelligence" unit took notice of my record. I was approached a few months later and told to apply for an opening as a drug dog handler. I said, "I'm interested but what's involved in applying?"

"Just apply." he said.

I did and was called in for an interview a couple of weeks later once the competition was posted. Two people that had previously held dog handler positions also applied, but it was apparent to me that I had been picked even before the position was posted. I got the job, and I never kissed anyone's ass to get it.

For training, I went to headquarters 2,700 miles away for about nine weeks to be trained on how to handle a drug dog. My dog had been pretty much trained already by the superintendent of the training division. He was a two-year-old yellow Lab, and he was very loyal to that instructor superintendent. My dog was very dominant and wanted nothing to do with me.

I had to overcome his dominance and get him to follow my demands and consider me the alpha dog in our relationship instead of him looking up to my supervisor. It was a tedious task, and he bit me several times but the scars have since faded. Finally after a hell of a lot of repetitious practicing and several dog bites to my hands, he accepted me as his master and did something I've never seen a dog do. I doubt if anyone has. He walked over to his past master (my superintendent and instructor) and during a group practice, he pissed on his past master's leg. The master looked down and saw his light blue coveralls had a six-by-eight-inch wet spot just above his shoe. I laughed my ass off and went over to my dog to give him a big hug and a reward. "GOOD BOY! GOOD BOY!" From that point on, he pretty much ignored my instructor.

While training, I trained alongside three other fellows from different parts of the country. One of them was given a dog that had a terrible habit. It involved the "hides", which are little baggies filled with marijuana that we'd hide for the dogs to find. This particular dog found the hides as fast as any other dog, but instead of giving them back to his master, he would swallow them. Then at the end of the day, we all had to walk around the two-acre field where we trained the dogs and look for dog shits with little cloth bags sticking out of them.

This was because we were accountable for every bit of the marijuana. You can't simply say, "The dog ate it." I suppose the dog might have got a little buzzed, but I don't know for sure. There was no evidence of it. Once you found one of the hides, you'd turn it over to the guy who trained that dog. He had to take it inside, wash the poop off, take the marijuana out, weigh and record it, and put it back in stock.

That particular dog was really screwed up. He had another bad habit too. It happened when he was at airports checking baggage on conveyor belts. The dogs would run back and forth over top of the suitcases on a moving conveyor belt. If they detected drug scent, they would immediately react by scratching and biting at the suspected suitcase so you'd pull the bag off the belt to check it for drugs. The dog would jump down and still go after the suitcase because he viewed it as a toy and wanted to play.

If that particular dog had to have a shit, he did it right on the belt in between suitcases. And this wasn't just occasionally; this was almost every time he checked bags at the airport. I'd be standing beside the conveyor belt watching the suitcases go by: one suitcase, another suitcase, another suitcase, then a dog shit, then another suitcase. Quite funny, but thankfully it was not my dog so it wasn't my problem.

One of the other dog handlers had a black lab that liked to eat poop or roll in it. So if we were in a field practicing with buried hides and the dog came across a big pile of cow poop, she would either roll in it or eat some of it. Apparently the dogs viewed that as a kind of a perfume when they rolled in it because they like the scent, and they wanted to smell like that. My dog didn't exhibit any bad habits, I'm proud to say.

Have you ever noticed that almost everybody who owns a dog will tell you that their dog thinks it is a person. That is incorrect. What is correct is that every dog thinks that you are a dog, and your dog determines whether it is you or he who is the top dog (alpha dog). I'll tell you right now that if your dog is sleeping on your bed with you, you are not the alpha dog.

I kept my dog on a strict diet and fed him once in the morning with premium dog food and water. However, my good wife thought that she would be kind to the dog and feed him some cheese one day. While at work my dog experienced diarrhea. When I got home that evening I asked my wife if she had fed my dog anything. She sheepishly looked at me and admitted she had given him some cheese. I sarcastically thanked her and asked her to please not do that in the future! I'm pretty sure she didn't, but sometimes she doesn't listen, especially when big brown begging eyes are telling her not to.

One time my knowledge as a dog handler helped me make my own getaway. My house was on a busy street and one evening three young guys were walking past and kicking the fence boards out of the fence next door. I wanted to confront them, but I didn't want them to know that I lived in the house next door, so I followed them for a few blocks. Then I approached them and blasted them for breaking boards on my neighbors' fences.

One of them picked up a big rock and threw it at me, narrowly missing the side of my head. I could actually feel the rock when it whizzed by my ear. That's when the adrenaline kicked in, and I lost it on them. I started to punch one of them and then wrestled with another one. The third guy took off his jacket and threw it on the ground and then came at me.

I had enough of an adrenaline jolt to overcome all three of them, and one ran away to a payphone to call the police for help. All of a sudden these tough-guy assholes were crying like babies to the cops. I doubt that the police would've taken their side when the odds were three against one, but I didn't want to take the chance. I picked up the jacket the guy dropped and took off with it to a vacant lot around some commercial buildings nearby.

When the fellow went to the pay phone to call the police I knew he was successful because in a very short period of time, a police dog unit was circulating around. I knew they were looking for me. Being a dog handler at the time, I was familiar with what a dog could find, and I knew the limits of what a dog handler would actually go through to find a subject. I simply went over a couple of eight-foot fences knowing full well that the dog handler would not do that. Good thing I took the jacket because it padded the top of the chain link fence when I went over it. By the time the cop went around the fence, they might lose the scent for a while, but they could eventually pick it up again.

If the dog handler actually went that far, the second fence would have changed his mind, and he would more than likely abandon the pursuit. He wouldn't know for sure if he was even on the right scent any more. I worked my way back home, zigzagging and taking abnormal shortcuts until I was sure no dog could trace me anymore.

Now that I had a jacket I was wondering to myself if that might be perceived as a robbery. It concerned me a lot, so the next day I mailed the jacket to the local police with a note explaining that while I was visiting my girlfriend's house (a lie I made up), three boys were damaging her fence. When I confronted them, they quickly turned violent. I mailed the package without postage because I figured it would be delivered for sure since it was addressed to the police with no return address. I didn't really care anyway.

I didn't take my dog when I went on training that wasn't dog related. One of my coworkers and I went on a training session a few hundred miles away. In order to break the monotony of the long drive, we decided to pick up a cold pack of beer and drink it on the way. Of course drinking in a government vehicle is strictly against policy, but when nobody's watching, things happen that probably should not happen.

By the time we got to our destination we were pretty drunk. My partner was driving there, and I was going to drive back the next day after the course was over. He told me that he was so hammered that he was seeing double and his vision was very blurry, so it's a good thing we made it to our hotel room. I was in no position to take over driving because I was just as drunk.

The training was rather boring and not much was retained by attending, so on the way back home we decided to buy another pack of beer. This time I was driving. It wasn't long before we started to feel the effects and again we got quite drunk, especially since the effects of the alcohol consumed the previous night probably hadn't worn off yet. In order to hide the evidence should we get stopped, we were throwing the empties out the window into the ditch. It wasn't something you'd expect to see from law enforcement officers in a company vehicle.

We were about an hour and a half from home when we drove through a small town where there was a police car parked on the side of the road. Crap!, I thought, If that cop decides to pull us over and check us, the smell of alcohol in our vehicle is so strong that there's no doubt in my mind we would have to take a breathalyzer reading. We would probably lose our jobs, especially if somebody saw us throwing beer bottles out the window while driving a marked company vehicle. Fortunately the police car was parked there because the cop had gone into a restaurant.

I did get stopped for speeding a few times while in my drug dog vehicle. I trained my dog to bark in a frenzy when policeman were approaching my door. While a cop was approaching, I would say, "Get him." Then the dog would start barking at the cop. As soon as they realized I was in law enforcement, they would let me go.

One time I was in court, and as soon as I finished giving evidence, I got a call from my alarm company saying the alarm at my home was going off. I had left all of my heroin, cocaine, marijuana, and hashish, and two firearms in a safe in my bedroom. While in court, things are more vulnerable in the car when it is in a parkade. I was driving crazy fast through traffic to get home as soon as I could and didn't notice two plainclothes cops in the car behind me. Once home they asked me, "What was the hurry?"

I explained my situation to them, but I don't think they believed me because one followed me into the house. I showed him my safe and pulled out all of my practice tools, drugs, and guns etc. This was my reason for driving so fast to get home. They accepted that, but for a few days I was worried that they would report the issue to my chief at work. They didn't.

While I'm on the subject of speeding tickets, I once got a speeding ticket was when I was living inland. I pleaded "not guilty". My case was that I could not have been speeding because my radar detector would have alerted me and it did not. I guess I was a bit too cocky because the judge called me a liar and said, "If you have a radar detector, you are a speeder. Guilty as charged!" I learned a lesson from that too. Don't say you have a radar detector in your car if you're contesting a speeding ticket. It won't go well.

While working at the border in the interdiction and intelligence division, I had the opportunity to be involved in a sting that involved one kilogram of opium that somebody had ordered by mail and was intercepted by officers in the mailroom. We worked in conjunction with the federal cops to arrange a sting.

There were several law-enforcement officers involved in four vehicles. The plan was to deliver the opium and then search the premises with a search warrant once the package had been delivered. We were staked out in a parking lot nearby, waiting for the postal truck to complete the delivery. Once it was delivered, we waited for another fifteen minutes or so to see if anybody came to pick up the drugs. However about five minutes later, the lady of the house exited the premises and drove away. This is why it's a good thing to have more people there than you might need.

We were now in a position of not knowing whether the kilo of opium was leaving with her or if it was still at the residence. A decision was made for one car to follow her until she was in a place where she could be pulled over safely. Then they would detain her until a search warrant could be secured. We used a heavy metal battering ram to bust the door open and had to locate the opium quickly in order to eliminate the need to pull the lady over at all.

When the guy with the battering ram hit the doorknob and smashed the door in, there was a small dog inside. That dog was so terrified by that intrusion that it ran past us like it was on fire, right between our legs and down the street. I'm sure that dog was never seen again.

The opium was very easy to find so the car sent to detain the lady was called off. Her husband was in the kitchen and had unwrapped the parcel. He had some small cooking pots on the stove. It appeared he was going to somehow render down the opium into smaller portions. There were two very young kids in that residence – one was a toddler in diapers. They were also clearly terrified by the invasion. They stayed in the house and did not follow the dog, but I bet you knew that.

The man was arrested and the children were taken into care by social services. The whereabouts of the dog remained unknown. If you have ever seen a dog that was afraid of fireworks run away, you'll know there's no telling how far or where they will go. Hopefully, this one ended up in a better home.

One time I was paged to attend a border crossing to check a truck that was on a lookout list for drugs. When I started to put my drug dog around the truck, he showed some interest underneath the driver's side. One of our interdiction and intelligence people was under the truck on the other side, so I got the dog to check the inside of the cab first.

When I put him inside the truck, he indicated on the seat as well. The customs inspector who was with me thoroughly searched the inside of the cab as well as underneath and could find nothing. I said, "Did you look underneath the truck because the dog showed some interest there before I put him in the cab." She confirmed she had already checked underneath and there was something there she wanted me to look at. She said she was not familiar with one of the parts of the undercarriage.

She took me over to the passenger side and when we looked under, she pointed out the catalytic converter and asked me if that was a normal thing on the bottom of a vehicle. I was down on my knees when I looked at that catalytic converter and said, "That's nothing to be concerned about. However, if you look on top of the gas tank there," and I pointed, "you will see a couple of kilos of drugs right on the top." They were hard to see because they were only slightly visible, and they were on the driver's side of the truck where the dog first indicated.

She looked at me and said, "You're fucking kidding, right?"

I said, "No I'm not kidding. I'll go get 'you' some help because I'm not crawling under there."

While she was under there digging them out, I called a couple of other members of the interdiction and intelligence team. They helped her get them all out. At the end of the search there were six kilograms of cocaine in a box. The driver was arrested and charged with smuggling cocaine. He pleaded "not guilty", and I had to go to court. The judge asked me about when the dog scratched on the seat, "Was it something the dog would have done if the occupant had merely set a rifle there since the dog was trained to find firearms as well."

I admitted, "Yes, it was possible." The accused had chosen to be judged by "judge alone" rather than a jury, which is why the judge asked the question that the defense attorney should have asked. The judge thanked me for my honesty. In giving further evidence, I indicated that when I looked underneath at the bottom of the truck from the passenger side, I could see what appeared to be cocaine on the top of the gas tank. I gave evidence that when the dog indicated on the seat, the accused could have had the drugs there first and then moved them to the gas tank when he was closer to the border. The bricks of cocaine may have fallen off of on the gas tank for a longer distance.

The accused was listening to me give evidence, and then he took the stand in an attempt to counter what I had said. In doing so, he said, "If there was cocaine on top of my gas tank, it would have slid off even in a short distance because the gas tank is sloped. If there was cocaine on it, it would have fallen out right away."

I was thinking, I wonder if this dumb ass knows he's corroborating my evidence. That really added credibility to my evidence and all I could do was grin. Earlier I mentioned that as a jail guard it was evident that some of the people inside really are not very intelligent. This kind of proved that theory, because if he was aware that the gas tank was sloped, he had knowledge that most people would not have. Do you know if your gas tank is sloped or level? I don't and I don't think the judge did either because the guy was found guilty and sentenced to six years in jail. The dog was credited for the bust, which I believe he deserved.

I was still working with the intelligence branch when I elected to go for a training session in another city for a conference with people in law enforcement from all over North America. It was called the Youth Gang Conference and was given by experts in every field of law enforcement to educate attendees on the methods of criminal activity used by foreign gangs. At that time, Japanese and Chinese mafia-type, well-organized gangs had the attention of law enforcement in addition to the American and Canadian gangs. The only thing different then than now, is that now there are more gangs than law enforcement is able to investigate.

The course was a four-day classroom study that I was happy to attend because I played hooky for most of it after checking in each day. My wife came with me, and we stayed at the host hotel where the conference was held. We met a lot of law enforcement people at the socials held afterward, and those socials were more interesting because information was exchanged on a personal basis. Informal one-on-one meetings always top classroom exchanges.

My wife and I sat at a supper table in a restaurant with a couple of city councilors, two FBI guys, and a federal cop accompanied by his wife. I sat between my wife and a councilor (Alderwoman Bev somebody). She was questioning all of us about the firepower (side arms) that we thought were necessary for cops. Her city was still carrying those Webley .38 caliber short-load revolvers. Of course the FBI guys said law enforcement should never carry anything less than a 9mm automatic pistol. I agreed and she was surprised when I told her I used to be a cop here in her city, and I thought their side arms were laughable.

I told her about a guy that was on the third-floor balcony of his apartment on a cold winter day. He was threatening people with a rifle and was shot by a cop with a Webley .38. He had enough warm clothing on to prevent the bullet from penetrating his skin. That's how useless their guns were.

I'm not sure if that actually ever happened, or if it was a story created by a frustrated cop who was so disappointed with his side arm that he felt the need to embellish a tad. I wanted to believe it was possible though, and I wanted her to believe it too. I think she did. Anyway, as it turned out, this Bev was on the Mayor's committee to study the feasibility of upgrading their police department firearms and the upgrades eventually came to fruition.

After dinner, my wife and I decided to return to the hotel before I got too liquored up to drive. The two FBI agents were staying at the same hotel and asked if they could hitch a ride back with us because the restaurant was too far away to walk. I was familiar with the city having been a cop there before. We were going west and stopped for a red light right behind an ambulance that was waiting for the light to change. Then all hell broke loose. Co-incidentally, we were very close to the rear door of a building occupied by the police department.

All of a sudden, the back doors of the ambulance violently flung open. Their patient jumped out and ran while the ambulance attendants were shouting for him to stop. The ambulance guys chased him, and the FBI guys in my back seat jumped out to help the ambulance guys. I jumped out too, and I don't even know why. Total chaos!

Everyone was shouting and that attracted the attention of two cops in uniform who had just exited their building. The patient was quickly restrained and all that was left to do was explain to the two local cops that we were all law enforcement officers and were assisting the ambulance attendants who very much appeared to be needing that assistance.

On occasion I worked at an international airport where there was a police dog endurance course, which I used for training my dog. I had to drive across the pathway of the commercial airline traffic to use it though. Once I got to the course, I used the mounds of dirt that hid me from the airport tower as a backstop for my bullets. I shot my pistol so that I would have fresh spent rounds to put in the training revolver that I used for training the dog. Had I been caught driving across the pathway of the jets, or even worse, shooting off a gun inside a major airport, I would've been in deep shit, especially in regards to firing the weapon.

I didn't realize the seriousness of driving across the pathway of the jets until I was showing a new dog handler the ropes. After I showed him the dog endurance course, he got caught driving across the pathway of the jets, and to my surprise, they pulled his airport driver's license. Probably to his surprise as well. That rendered him unable to drive his vehicle anywhere inside the area where the planes were contained. It was a short-term suspension, but he was reprimanded for it. Better him than me.

My drug dog was excellent at finding drugs, and in fact, I even searched for drugs at one of the local remand centers that housed prisoners. I didn't like that very much because as soon as I entered the complex with the dog, the convicts would all start to whistle just to irritate him. I just ignored it because to react was exactly what they were looking for.

My drug dog was extremely well trained. I never even needed a leash, but while working him on vehicles when traffic was close by, I used a leash as a precaution. He found a lot of drugs: cocaine, heroin, hashish, marijuana, and even firearms. The largest quantity he hit on was

6,000 pounds of hashish at an international airport. It's a well-known fact that sometimes bad guys will put out a hit on a drug dog that has significantly undermined their profits. I heard a rumor that my dog was a target because he was so good at his job.

He also found 100 grams of heroin in a shoe and grabbed onto it because he viewed these finds as toys. Then he shook the shit out of it. His teeth punctured the plastic bag, and there was heroin powder flying everywhere. I was taught that if something like that should ever happen, I needed to give him a shot of Narcan to counteract any effects of heroin. I gave him the shot and then rushed him to the veterinarian. He was there for a few hours until the vet determined he had not ingested enough of the loose powder to harm him.

Occasionally I would practice with other law-enforcement agencies. The one I preferred the most was with a cross-border dog handler. He used to come across and we worked in warehouses on my side and occasionally I'd go to his country and practice in their warehouses. I was on my way into their territory one day through one of their ports of entry, and when I approached the primary booth to get clearance from the inspector, he asked me if I had anything to declare.

I didn't know him and I didn't know what to say about all the drugs I had in my vehicle (for practice) as well as the two revolvers. I took the precautionary measure of telling him I had some marijuana, cocaine, heroin, hashish, and a couple of revolvers. I'd bet money you won't be able to find anybody that can make a declaration like that and still be permitted to carry on when crossing a border, let alone someone who actually had all that stuff in the vehicle.

One time, the federal police called me to do a search for weapons and explosives on a flight that British royalty was about to board an hour or two later. They wanted to make sure there were no explosives on that plane because it wouldn't have been good for them if a plane carrying royalty blew up before or after leaving the country.

I told the federal cop that my dog wasn't trained to detect explosives, only gunpowder residue. However, he asked me to run the dog by all the suitcases and luggage anyway, in case someone from their plane crew was paying attention. My guess is that this exercise was performed to cover his butt in case somebody important enough to complain was watching to see if it was done. If the plane exploded after take-off, he would likely try and blame me for not finding the explosives.

My dog and I once checked a new Mercedes at a major crossing, and I had the dog run through the inside of the car. The car belonged to a known drug dealer, and I assumed that he, at one time, had some drugs on the passenger seat. The reason I say that is because my dog scratched the seat, which is an indication that drugs were there previous to my search. I checked the car and the seat pretty thoroughly, but there was nothing to be found.

Unfortunately the dog's toenails hadn't been clipped for a while, and he made a tear on the seat of this brand-new

Mercedes. The fellow who owned it was inside the building waiting for me to finish and did not see the dog do it, so I hid the tear with the seatbelt. The fellow was released and obviously he didn't know how the tear got there because we never heard back from him.

I didn't give a shit anyway because drug dealers usually have enough money to fix things like that. Besides, if I were blamed for it, I simply would've told him to file a claim, which would have taken several months to settle.

Another time I was checking a warehouse, and I had my dog run along the top of some cardboard boxes that were stacked about eight feet high. They formed a run along the top for about 60 feet. When he got to the end of the row he didn't know what to do and looked down at me for guidance. He had so much trust and faith in me that when I held up my arms for him to jump down, he did. What I wasn't expecting was that his dick hit me on the lips because I caught him too low. That was pretty disgusting, and I did a lot of spitting for a while. The customs inspector who was watching got quite a laugh out of that.

The only thing that terrified that dog was noisy kids who were pestering him. If I was sitting in my chair at home, he would jump up onto my lap for me to protect him. He weighed over 60 pounds so it looked a bit ridiculous.

I was at a truck terminal one day that was a bonded warehouse. That is a warehouse that is controlled by customs until imported merchandise is cleared. I was bullshitting with one of the customs inspectors who was working there. The tailgate of my truck was down, so if I needed the dog, all I had to do to get his attention was wave my arm from an outward position toward my chest.

When the dog saw this (and he was always watching me), he would jump out of the truck, run over to me and stand in a heel position to my right, looking up at me for further direction. While I was BS'ing, I didn't realize that I was talking with my hands. The dog saw the movement, reacted, and showed up at my side. He was so well trained and that gave me a chuckle. I looked down at him and said, "What are you doing here? Go back to the truck, KENNEL!" It was a command, and he immediately left my side and jumped back into the truck.

I got called out to a busy border crossing in the middle of the night to clear a bus with a rock band on board. There were six long-haired guys on the bus that were directed to sit on the curb outside while their bus was checked for drugs. I don't know what band they were, but they looked like a bunch of dopers. I was in the bus with my dog, running him through everything, and these guys were waiting patiently. They were sitting in a nice row on the curb just ahead of the bus. It was about 3:00 a.m., so my dog didn't have time to have a dump before I left home. As a result, he wasn't working very effectively.

I knew something was wrong but didn't act on it. Anyway the dog figured enough was enough. He left the bus and ran over to a grassy area right at the end of the row where these guys were sitting and had a dump beside the last guy. I was with another border inspector on the bus at the time, and I looked at him and said laughingly, "Look, my dog just had a crap right beside that last guy," and we both laughed. The Inspector who was with me blurted out, "What's one more pile of shit!" We both laughed again.

Another time I was checking a cruise ship and my dog was showing signs that he needed to void. I mentioned that to one of the ship's crew. He told me to take the dog into the kitchen where there is a place the dog could take a shit. Whaaat! In the kitchen? Sure enough, there was a room adjacent to the kitchen about twelve feet wide and twenty feet long with an opening to the outside of the ship. The kitchen crew throws leftovers and kitchen scrap in there, and when enough piles up, they use a big shovel to push it out the opening. They don't even need to lift the shovel up because there was no ledge under the doorway. It goes straight out into the ocean with very little effort.

I remember working at the airport as an interdiction and intelligence officer. A guy came in on a plane with a shitload of indicators that he could be a drug mule (a guy who brings in drugs for other people). There were enough indicators to warrant a strip search, so one was done. During that strip search, the inspector who detained the fellow noticed the guy's asshole had signs of redness and swelling. Yes, they were told to turn around, bend over, and spread their cheeks. The redness was an indicator that the guy might have shoved condoms or balloons filled with heroin or cocaine up his butt to avoid detection, so in he went to the hospital for an X-ray. The X-ray showed he had a quantity of what appeared to be drug filled condoms showing in his bowels. Now we had to guard him until he passed them. For the longest time, he didn't want to have a crap to void the drugs from his bowels.

What we needed here was some creativity to get him to shit. What would be better than a greasy hamburger? Yes, that should work, so we bought a large, greasy burger for him and some fried chicken for us. Hamburgers don't make you hungry when you smell them, but fried chicken does, so before we ate the chicken, we blew the scent into his room.

It worked like a charm, and he finally ate the damn burger. About 20 minutes later he had to poop. In order to catch the condoms, we used a wooden hospital toilet with a metal catch basin that slid into grooves under the seat. The hospital did not have the newest inventions like a catch toilet that allows liquids to pass but catches solids.

I went into the room with the fed whose job it was to weigh and record the quantities. The smuggler wasn't permitted to shit unless it was either in his pants or in that metal pot under the wooden chair. Cleaning off the condoms was one job I would never sign up for because the poop had to be cleaned off before they were weighed. I don't remember how many condoms there were, but enough pings hit the metal pot to make a sound like a bell ringer's padded hammer with the velocity of a slow shooting machine gun, and STINK! Wow did it ever stink!

Since my dog was part of the family when not working, my youngest son took him out for walks on occasion. He was told never to let the dog "off leash". One day he let the dog off leash a few hundred feet from the house thinking he was doing the dog a favor. He found out very quickly that his decision to do that was something he'd never forget for the rest of his life. A cat ran out in front of the dog. The dog chased it and was killed by a lady driving an SUV. She was devastated, my son and I and the rest of the family were as well. That ended my position as a dog handler.

I was moved to another position within the interdiction and intelligence umbrella until that unit was overhauled. I remained there for several months, and during that time, we did a tremendous amount of surveillance. In one instance we had two cars surveilling one business in the downtown area in a location that attracted a lot of street people or homeless types.

Those folks were always interesting to watch. Occasionally, we could see them doing things that were not entirely legal but also not worth exposing our location for, such as shooting up with drugs or pissing in doorways. One team was in a black van with blacked out windows. The other was in a cheesy-looking car that looked anything but law-enforcement. We were never in uniform so remained fairly incognito.

One of the guys decided to spice things up a little bit. On his way to the stakeout location, he had driven by a dead skunk on the road. He just saw it out of the corner of his eye. He could still smell skunk scent when driving by so came up with an idea. The next day while on route to the stakeout location, he brought a plastic bag and a box.

He put the dead skunk in the plastic bag and then put it in the box. Then he put the box in his trunk and brought it to the stakeout site.

None of the businesses were open yet, so there was not very much pedestrian traffic, which gave him the opportunity to put the box in one of the doorways just off the sidewalk. As we had anticipated, one of the homeless people saw an opportunity. Somebody had left a box there that might have something valuable in it. Surely that must be what was going through his mind.

We could all see this "porch bandit" bend down to open the box and check the contents. I don't know why he didn't smell it sooner, but as soon as he did, he came running out of there cussing and swearing. He had both fingers up flipping off the bird to anybody he could see because he thought for sure somebody was watching him and had set him up for this gag. He wasn't wrong, and it was a good laugh.

When my employer decided to downsize the Interdiction and Intelligence division, a number of us were reassigned to being uniformed officers again. I thought that if I had to go back to working on the line, I would put in for a transfer to a nice, laid-back, quiet port and avoid the hectic pace. I put in for a transfer to a port 600 miles away where I could enjoy the low traffic volume and put my feet up on a desk and chill. Turned out it wasn't as slow and relaxed as I anticipated, but it was still significantly quieter.

One evening I was working at the border of that laid-back port, and a charter bus full of tourists came to our crossing. The procedure was to board the bus and do primary questioning on every individual on the bus. Of course, I didn't follow that procedure. Instead, I would just take hold of the driver's microphone and ask that anyone who was bringing anything back over their exemption to please put up their hand.

I told them what their exemptions were and exaggerated what the penalties were for false declarations. Then I repeated my request for them to put their hands up if they were over their exemptions or they would face the music when I checked them. I had no intention of checking them individually, but I found my questioning to be far easier and faster than unloading the bus and talking to everyone separately.

There was a guy sitting in the front row facing me. He was about 25 or 30 years old. He had a small bottle of whiskey over his exemption. He thought that he'd be a funny man and guzzle it down in front of me so that I wouldn't collect duty on it. Next thing I knew, he upchucked all over me. My shirt was covered in vomit, but I kept my cool and told the bus driver to park. I instructed him to unload every piece of luggage on the bus and then have every passenger bring their own luggage inside so that I could check each and every one of them.

The coworkers with me at the time realized how pissed off I was, so they asked me if I needed any help, and I said, "No, I will do it myself when I get out of the shower."

So I had a shower and took my time, and then I went through the luggage of every individual on the bus, keeping them there for over three hours. I'm sure that fellow was not in for a very good time on the ride home because the other passengers wanted to kill him. Hopefully, he learned a lesson from the situation he had created.

I was working one afternoon shift when one of the law officers from the other side came over to have coffee. When we got the cameras installed at the port to read license plates, his curiosity got the best of him. I went to the booth when he drove up, and after chatting a bit, he said, "I wonder if that camera would still read my license plate if I went through here really, really fast."

I found that idea crazy but interesting and said, "I don't know. Why don't you try it." He was not one to walk away from a challenge, so he drove back to the other side of the border, and when there was no traffic, he approached our port in his car at close to 50 mph.

Our port was situated off-center from the highway, so in order to stay on the highway, he had to make a sharp left turn immediately after passing the building. There was a propane tank on the side of the hill just to the left of where he would hit if he went straight through. At that speed, he missed the turn. He could not stop before reaching the hill, which was grass but now had a layer of snow on it. He went up the hill and about 25 feet past the propane tank before he could slow down enough to make a turn and drive back down the snowy hill onto the roadway on the other side of the propane tank.

I'm sure he was white knuckling it, but from where we were watching, it was hilarious. We were laughing so hard we had tears. Things could have been a whole lot different if he'd run into the propane tank! There would have been a lot of explaining to do on both of our parts. The tracks in the snow looping the propane tank were quite noticeable but were never questioned by management. Sometimes it's best not to ask.

The same individual came around to visit me another time when I was working night shift alone. We got to talking about guns. He was going to show me how to clean his pistol because it needed cleaning anyway. He took the pistol out of the holster, handed it to me, and I cleaned and lubricated it under his step-by-step instructions. Of course, the first thing I did was unload the pistol and check for any shell that might have been in the chamber. He also showed me how to disassemble it and clean the pieces separately. I did it exactly the way that he said and loaded it again and gave it back to him. Now the creepy part starts.

The officer was soon called back to one of the towns just south of the port. An alarm had gone off in a small bar down there, and he went to investigate. The owner of the bar lived close to it, and he was also there investigating. The owner was armed with a rifle.

The officer left right after I had re-loaded his pistol and given it back. Crap, I hope he won't need it in case I screwed up while handling it. When he arrived at the bar, he did not recognize the owner and the owner did not recognize the officer. It was dark outside. The officer shouted out, " POLICE DEPARTMENT, DROP THE WEAPON NOW!" The bar's owner still had the rifle but might not have heard him. He was old, probably hard of hearing, and obviously sight challenged so I can understand that.

Over the confusion, the officer fired a shot killing the owner of the bar with the gun that I had just cleaned and a bullet I had just put in the clip after putting it back together. It was creepy that my DNA was probably on that bullet. After that, the officer received several death threats because people felt the shooting was not warranted. The bar's owner was a very popular fellow. The officer thought he'd best "get the hell out of Dodge" so to speak. He then quit that department and joined a police department further south just to escape threats to his life.

On another night, I was working alone and a camper bus with six individuals came through. To me it looked like they would be a good secondary examination for drugs or weapons. For my own safety, I had all but one of them go inside the office and sit down in the foyer while I checked the vehicle. I took the driver with me in case there were any compartments that I was unable to open or anything of that sort.

While I was checking the bus, the guys working on the other side of the border tried to phone me but could not get an answer. They knew I was not armed. I was pretty good friends with all the officers from both sides, so they thought they should come and investigate.

When they got to the primary booth and looked inside, they could see five guys wandering around in the foyer waiting for their vehicle to be examined. I glanced out the window of the bus occasionally to see what they were up to inside and noticed my counterparts approaching and brandishing their handguns. They were right beside the primary booth with guns raised ready to fire.

I thought to myself, Holy shit, they think that these guys have done something to me. I quickly got off the bus at which time another one of their officers came around the other side of the building with his gun out and pointing straight ahead until he saw me. The others saw me about the same time.

As soon as they recognized me, they said, "What's going on? We tried to call you and we didn't get an answer."

I said, "I was just checking this vehicle so I had those guys go sit inside and wait. Apparently they got a little restless and started walking around."

Had it been a situation where I was actually hijacked, they could have been in quite a compromising position due to the fact they had no authority on our side of the border. Still it reinforces the cliché of "Brothers in blue". It was truly appreciated!

Part Ten:
Final Years at the Border 'Inland'

I'VE NEVER BEEN a "yes man", and believe me, the federal government has an abundance of them. Have you ever heard of the "Peter Principle"? Look it up. It is on the net and defined as "a concept in management which observes that people in the hierarchy tend to rise to their level of incompetence. An employee is promoted based on their success in previous jobs until they reach a level at which they are no longer competent as skills in one job do not necessarily translate to another." (Laurence J. Peter)

Laurence Johnston Peter was a Canadian educator and "hierarchiologist" best known to the general public for the formulation of the Peter principle. Wikipedia

Born: September 16, 1919, Vancouver

Died: January 12, 1990, Palos Verdes Estates, California, United States

Education: Washington State University

Known for: Peter principle

That being said, I was at loggerheads with management continuously because if they came up with something that I thought was stupid, I told them.

I had never been a proponent of unions until I was so furious that a fellow worker died at work because management wanted to save a few dollars. A higher budget might not have saved his life, but a co-worker might have. Customs ports, particularly isolated ones, are dangerous. This worker might have lived if he had someone working with him when he suffered a serious medical condition, passed out, hit his head on the furniture, and bled on the floor.

That's how we found him when we started our shift. We tried to revive him. The ambulance took 40 minutes to reach the port. My fellow worker and I gave him CPR the entire time after he stopped breathing. When the ambulance arrived, they didn't take over. They loaded him, but we kept up with the CPR. He died before we reached the hospital.

I was furious with the manager who wouldn't put two people on shift at night. Night shifts are far more dangerous than other shifts, so allowing single-person shifts was irresponsible. I called that manager the next day and told him, "I hope you're happy that you saved a few dollars by running one-person shifts. You can be happier now because you don't have to pay wages to the guy whose death you might have caused."

In the past, I had argued with this particular manager many times. There was no doubt in my mind he was the perfect example of someone appointed using the "Peter

Principle". I made it my goal from that point on to run as president of my branch of the customs union. I won the position and was notified while having dinner with that same manager and a chief from the local head office, as well as the current union president (the guy I was running against). There was another shop steward there as well. I was there because I was the shop steward who represented my port.

Once we all heard I won, I just couldn't hold back. I looked over at the district manager and said to him, "You better be prepared for a fight because I'm going to give you one!" The look on his face was one that showed he might have been taken back by my remark, and it apparently irritated him. Exactly what I wanted to do. I wanted to put that bastard through as much grief as possible while doing his job. I wanted to push him into a nervous breakdown.

Every time a "watch for" was issued that specified "armed and dangerous", I advised my co-workers to refuse to work under the regulations defined by the government's own labor code. I didn't know if anyone had the courage to do it, so I took it upon myself to do the first one when an "armed and dangerous" watch for was issued.

It happened on a day when two inspectors had booked off sick so an overtime shift was necessary. It wasn't my turn to scoop an overtime shift, but I convinced others to refuse it so I could "refuse to work" as per the labor code. The supervisor knew of my intention, so when she called me at home to offer the shift, I had my wife answer the phone. My wife told her I was not home but that I would report for work on overtime.

She told my wife to tell me that I would be working alone, probably hoping I might refuse the shift like all the others she had called. I give credit to my co-workers who passed up the overtime so I could take a stand in the interest of safety. I truly appreciated that they did that.

I guess my supervisor figured that she had covered her butt by telling my wife that. She expected my wife to pass that message on to me, but I instructed her to say that she forgot. My supervisor had a hunch that I would show up to work and do the work refusal. She was normally off shift at 4:00 p.m., but when my shift started four hours later at 8:00 p.m., she was still there waiting for me to see if I would commit to my threat.

When I walked into the office she approached me and said, "You know you're working alone." I asked her if the armed and dangerous lookout had been dealt with or cancelled and she said, "No it hasn't been." So I said, "In that case I refuse to work under the legislation that protects me under the labor code." The labour code also states that once an individual refuses to work, no one else is supposed to work in that position until the issue is resolved.

I then went outside and put pylons up to stop all traffic because I was officially closing the border crossing in both directions. The lookout involved an individual that was allegedly on his way in our direction. He was armed and dangerous and was expected to come through our isolated port. Not too many border crossings are as isolated as this particular location was, so I was well within my rights. Police and ambulance were often over an hour away, and at that time, we were not armed.

The supervisor then called over to the next closest port about a two-hour drive away to have her own supervisor come to our port to assist and allow traffic to continue to flow. Supervisors will breach the government's own regulations simply because they can with no consequences.

The chief showed up with one of the customs inspectors from the port two hours away. I was shocked this inspector would have the nerve. What really pissed me off was that this gal was my secretary in the union. That was embarrassing! She was pretty much shunned by everybody after that, and I dismissed her as my union secretary. She ended her own career with customs some time after that.

Anyway, they did open the port to allow traffic through. According to the labor code, it was my obligation to stay there until somebody from the labor code office came out to investigate and declare the refusal safe or unsafe. It took several hours for their representative to finally get to our destination. I believe she flew in from elsewhere in the country and then had to rent a car to drive the one-hour distance from the airport to us. As expected, she declared that there was no danger because no threat had actually surfaced, no bad guys had showed up, and nobody had been injured even though the potential was there. Sawmills that have dust hazards, which cause explosions, are never permitted to remain open until the hazards are eliminated. To me, this was no different.

I am inclined to believe that she was instructed to rule that it wasn't warranted for fear of opening up doors across the country at all other ports of entry. That was exactly my intention! She interviewed me for at least two hours, so from the time I got to work and about five or six hours of waiting for her to show up and two more for the interview, I accumulated a pretty good paycheck from the overtime generated.

The labor representative who interviewed me pissed me off a bit too, because I knew she was lying. When the interview was finished, I wished her farewell and said, "Be careful driving back because there are a lot of animals out there, and I really wouldn't want to see you get killed." I said it in a sarcastic tone and gave her a threatening glare. That appeared to trouble her. I was happy with that result.

She caught the sarcasm, as did the chief that showed up from the other port and he voiced concerns about my tone, but I said, "It wasn't sarcasm. I was truly concerned about her safety." I left the port and laughed about it all the way home.

A day or so before I did that work refusal, I phoned the union head office to talk to one of their technical people to reaffirm my rights under the labor code. The union advisor told me that I should not risk doing the refusal because there was a possibility I could be fired. I said, "I am going to do it anyway because the labor code specifically prohibits the employer from exercising any retaliation. I hope the union is going to back me up if that does happen." I hung up.

I don't think it was too long, perhaps two weeks, until my next work refusal. I got a call from law enforcement on the other side of the border telling me there was a murder about 500 feet from their port of entry. Apparently an individual who lived in the house close to them was shot and killed and the murderer was at large.

I thought this was a pretty damn good reason for refusing to work once again. This time it was not just a "watch for". This time it was a murder committed by a man living close by who was armed with a rifle or pistol. The safest and most probable way for him to escape would be to go into another country that is in close proximity to where he committed the murder.

This time there were no supervisors at work, so I told my co-worker to go and put pylons up for the approaching traffic to stop them from crossing. I would do the same on the other side to stop all traffic from the other direction. Then I phoned our counterparts and told them that I had declared our workplace a danger because there was a murderer at large in the area.

That shut down was effective enough to keep the border closed for several hours before a supervisor showed up and before someone from the Labor Code Department could come out and interview me once again. I was wondering how they were going to find that situation "safe to work in" and as it turned out, they really didn't. I think they probably heard about gunshots and a murderer running around and didn't want to risk their lives coming out to investigate it or they didn't want to take a chance that they may be forced to rule that it wasn't safe.

Anyway, against all regulations, I was then ordered to go home with pay. The order was totally in violation to the legislation, and no labor code employee even bothered to come out. However, I was contacted by one of them over the phone. Apparently they were under the impression that my work refusals were frivolous. I do not believe they were. It is clearly stated that the employer cannot carry out any disciplinary action on any employee that is acting under the safety regulations of the code.

While I am on things that happened at that particular isolated port, one day I was working with a student inspector. The district manager had contacted internal affairs to come out and interview me to see if there was any way they could discipline me or dismiss me. A young lady from headquarters internal affairs showed up to do the interview. I knew we would be meeting in the office so I set my chair up high and lowered the one she was going to be sitting in behind the desk. I read somewhere that this has a psychological effect on the person in the lower position so I planned on making this an enjoyable session.

Boy, did it turn out to be enjoyable. My luck came to fruition once again. The inspector I was working with encountered an individual at the primary booth who told her he was on his way to straighten out the black population in the area. Not only was this a "hate type of referral", but it was very unusual. And yes, my co-worker characterized this as a valid reason to refer the guy to secondary for further examination.

While she was searching his car, she looked under the driver's seat and noticed a clock with black tape around it and several wires coming out of it. She immediately came in and asked me to step out for a minute, which I did, enabling me to disrupt the interview.

She explained to me that she was concerned it might be a bomb. I told her to lock the individual up in the cell in the back and then walk up the highway and close it down to traffic once again. This was my third border closure in a matter of a couple of months and done right under the nose of internal affairs. I was already getting the attention of top federal managers, so this should really get them to take note.

I told my co-worker that once she closed the highway, she should walk over to the duty-free store across the street and inform them of a possible bomb threat and have them keep their distance from our office. I also told her to stay at the duty-free store with the employees there in order to stay out of danger. Then I went back into the office to see the internal affairs lady and told her she better get the hell out of there right away because there was a possibility that a bomb was in the car outside.

She took my words very seriously. She pretty much ran out to her rental car and drove off screeching the tires. It was the end of that interview. For her, it wasn't a successful interview, but for me it certainly was.

I then walked down to see our counterparts on the other side of the border, stopping all traffic and putting up more pylons. When I walked into their office and told them I was shutting down the border again for the third time, they all thought it was great. Besides, they were not in any danger, and now they could take some time off and wait until our bomb unit arrived. That would be a few hours because they had to fly in from 600 miles away and then drive an hour to get to our port.

Since "buddy" with the alleged bomb was now in a locked cell in the back of the office, I thought it would be interesting if he did have a bomb in there – especially if it went off and he was the only victim. That's not very compassionate, but it would be good karma.

What I didn't know was that a police sergeant from the closest town 25 or so miles away showed up to see what was going on. The sergeant saw the pylons on the road blocking traffic in both directions, and he assumed that my partner and I were at our counterparts' office on the other side of the border.

He drove straight over there. I told him what was going on and he said, "Well, where is the guy who was in the car?"

I told him, "He's in lock up. That way if the building blows up, there will be no court and no charges so no loss. Besides he's in a cell on the opposite side of the building, so he should be all right."

The cop looked at me like I was nuts and said, "Well we've got to get him out of there." I was thinking to myself, KEENER!

I thought I better go with him just to cover my ass. Besides, I knew the combination to the door, I had a key to the cell, and I knew where everything was. The cop wasn't familiar with our building. We drove over in his car to the back door, and I ran inside to pull the guy out and put him in the back of the police car. Then we went back to their office and waited until the bomb squad arrived. The cop got bored after a few hours and left with our prisoner.

About five hours later, the bomb squad showed up and looked under the seat. They found that it was just an alarm clock with black tape on it and a bunch of wires but not a bomb. Oh well, no bomb, no explosion, no excitement. But hey, at the end of it all, I got rid of the internal affairs lady! It also reinforced my issues about refusing to work because she certainly didn't want to hang around. Things couldn't have gone any better if I'd planned it. To my credit, a few people thought I did!

I did know that I was a proverbial pain in the ass to management as a union activist who was causing a tremendous amount of trouble for them. I heard that the regional manager was researching the possibility of booking me off with a "mental disability order" issued by management. I told you he was a stupid bastard!

Apparently, they think they can do that if they feel an employee is unstable and still working. When my superintendent informed me that the regional manager was coming out to interview me on my next day shift, my "spidey senses" went into high gear. I could see the writing was on the wall, and I knew where he was trying to go, starting with that interview. As soon as she informed me he was coming, I told her that I was booking off sick for an indefinite period of time because of all the stress I had endured in the past couple of months.

Then I stayed away for 96 work hours comprised of two, four-day shifts of 48 hours each. When I got back 20 days later, I put in a claim under Worker's Compensation benefits in order to get my full pay without using any sick leave. There wasn't anything they could do about it other than refer me for a psychological assessment by a Worker's Compensation Board psychologist to determine whether or not I was suffering from post-traumatic stress disorder (PTSD). I was good with that because I knew I had it. Over the years, I have sought help from psychologists to learn how to understand it. It doesn't go away, but I am able to understand why some of my emotions are uncontrollable. Many of the traumas I have suffered are described in this book. Well, not all of them. Some were too graphic to write about.

They actually did refer me to a Worker's Compensation psychologist. They had to fly me with all expenses paid to where the head office for Worker's Compensation was located. They had to pay me overtime for the entire trip from my home and back as well as all meals, airline tickets, my travel time, vehicle mileage, and all the time that I spent there getting interviewed.

I thought the interview went really well, and it appeared to me to be very much in my favor. The reason I say that is because I was able to shed tears when the psychologist was interviewing me. I won't say whether the tears were real or not, but she found me to be genuine and my claim to be valid. My employer was ordered to pay me full pay for all the shifts that I missed without docking any of my sick time. Now, management was in a position to be set up for harassment if they tried anything else. I pretty much had them by the short hairs.

During that time, I flew to headquarters often and was paid a pretty good mileage rate to drive to a large airport four hours away. All my hotels, meals, and mileage were covered by the union and included in my work time in regards to retirement benefits just as if I had actually been at work.

I was away so much that I actually forgot to go to work for a shift that I was scheduled for. No one called me to see why I wasn't coming in. When I went to work the next day a co-worker asked me if I was away on union business. "No, it was my day off." He told me I was scheduled to work. "Oh shit! Don't say anything about it to anyone, I just forgot to check the schedule." He said it wasn't a problem," so I managed to scam a free day off.

When I was away, however, I had lots of time to talk to other presidents of our national union. I explained to them how all this refusal stuff worked and as a result they started to do them. They did multiple refusals in the eastern part of the country.

When I was working at the port one day, I was called by a union steward at one of the main crossings who told me that police officials on the other side of the border had chased a car towards them. Once the occupant of that car realized he was boxed in by traffic, he jumped out of his car and started shooting at them. My union members there, tried to get all the traffic out of the way in case the fugitive decided to hijack someone, but clearing traffic out of the way was an impossible task. So the steward called me and said, "What should I do?"

I said, "Go and tell all of those inspectors to leave their outside booths, go inside, and refuse to work under the labor code. You are all within your rights." They knew I had done that a few times, so they took my advice.

That border crossing, the biggest in our area, was shut down for several hours. I believe the fellow in the car who was shooting at the officers was apprehended before he was able to enter our country, but that did not diminish the potential for immediate danger.

During my time on the union, I was lucky enough to do a lot of lobbying with big name politicians at the federal level and had several discussions with at least three of them who were political appointees, all from different political parties. Then when the outgoing party was defeated, the incoming party decided to eliminate single-person shifts completely. The union, through lobbying, was able to include the arming of officers into future training and firearms for all border officers across the country. I was fortunate enough to be able to try out several firearms made by different manufacturers that the government was considering purchasing. The manufacturers were all told to submit their best price and the most beneficial offer was supposed to be the one chosen. The firearms instructor asked me which of them I preferred. I told him, "I liked them all!"

When I was trying out firearms we were told the bidding structure was not a fair contract. The federal police were equipped with 9mm Smith & Wessons, so it appeared that our management by-passed all bids except the Smith and Wesson Company. That was discovered only because this particular firearms instructor slipped up and told us. They figured they could sneak it in so that they would simply need only to deal with one gun manufacturer and increase the orders of 9mm Smith & Wessons. Likely the older guns currently out on issue might eventually be dumped onto border officers.

So the new government got caught trying to circumvent its bidding process. After a few months of waiting for bids and trying out weapons, they had to re-post the bid solicitation so that a fair bidding competition was honored. In doing so, a different company won the bidding. The arming of all officers was scheduled to take a number of years, and I retired before it was fully implemented.

Some strange things happened at the port because there was a farm not too far away on the other side and they were raising emus. One day, one of those emus came through the primary booth and looked at us through the window. "What are we going to do with a damn emu?"

What were our choices? Welcome it to our country? Refuse entry due to agricultural concerns? Kill it and eat it? So many options! We settled on "leave the damn thing alone and hope it goes back home". Eventually it did leave on its own.

Once there was a skunk standing right in the middle of the road where the cars to be cleared through customs needed to drive. The next car waiting at the stop sign chose to wait it out, and I appreciated that. No need to create a scent storm.

We visited and socialized with our counterparts at the border quite a bit. One time they got a giant slingshot with elastics that pulled back about six feet, and they started firing water balloons at us during times when the traffic was slow. We didn't have a slingshot, but we took away a lot of apples that were prohibited from entering our country so we threw the apples back at them and they littered the road. The broken balloons hardly showed at all. I deem that as a win.

Another time we saw a skunk approaching, so we started throwing apples at it, and it went back to the other side across the street from our counterparts. I phoned them and Inspector Marge was working. She was a firearms instructor and thought this might perhaps be some good practice. She took a bead on the skunk, fired one shot, and nailed it. However, somebody called in a "shots fired" complaint and she received a written reprimand for it.

Then there was a pheasant just outside the door on the traffic side. I tied a string to a toolbox and propped the door open a little bit with it. Then I put a corncob down to try and lure the pheasant inside. After some time, it was curious enough to come in and investigate. I pulled on the string, releasing the door, and I had the pheasant trapped inside the office. That turned out to be not such a good idea because this goddamn bird was flying all over the inside and crashing into the windows and the curtains. It was creating quite the commotion. My work partner went around to open the back door, and we were able to herd the bird out of the building.

I was what you might call an old school customs inspector. Back in the day, if we found something that was suspected to be drugs we would lick out finger, stick it in the powder, and taste it. That was before meth was circulating. The cocaine taste is similar to aspirin if you have ever chewed one. It has a bitter taste. Although we were warned plenty of times not to do this, I did not heed the warnings.

While searching the trunk of a vehicle, I found a small bag full of a white powder. So I did the old "dip the finger and taste the drug trick", and before too long I was high. "Damn it!" I sure didn't expect that! I couldn't let the boss know what I had just done because it wouldn't have gone well. It would have generated extreme procedure reports, and I certainly didn't want to go that route. So instead, I went into the office and told her I was feeling really sick and I had to go home. As it turned out, it was meth and not cocaine. I had tasted cocaine using that method before, and it never had any effect on me so I thought it was the fastest way to determine if I had a drug bust or not. Lesson learned!

I was working with a partner on an afternoon shift at an isolated port when a young man came walking up to the primary booth. He had been drinking heavily, and while he was drunk, he also had some medical issue going on. I verbally prodded him a little because something wasn't quite right about his actions and his demeanor. His eyes appeared sunken and abnormal even for a drunk.

Eventually he told me he needed to take his insulin shot. I asked him where his insulin was. He said, "It's at home and I need to take it soon because I'm a diabetic, and I need a shot now."

I said, "Where do you live?"

He said, "About three miles up the road. I'm a farm-hand there, and I live in a shack behind the house."

I said, "Can I phone someone and have them bring your insulin here?"

He said he lived alone. I decided to leave my co-worker and used the company vehicle to drive him home. He was on the verge of passing out when I put him in the passenger seat of the port vehicle and sped off. On the way to his house I managed to get some directions to the exact location of his residence as well as how much insulin he would need and how he took it. He said he needed 10 mg and the syringes were in the cupboard, but his insulin was in the fridge and that he took the needle in the stomach.

By the time I got him home he was ready to pass out, but I managed to get him into the house. Then he did pass out. I had worked part-time as an ambulance attendant before, but I never really learned a lot about diabetics. One thought that came to mind was that usually a patient is his own best doctor, and if he was telling me he needed insulin I was going to assist him in getting it. I found his insulin in the fridge and the needles in the cupboard. I loaded the syringe up with 10 mg of insulin and pulled up his shirt. Then I stuck the needle in his gut and gave him the shot he said he needed.

I had my co-worker call an ambulance when I left the port, and I was able to direct the ambulance workers to the residence by communicating with them through my co-worker by radio. They showed up and we loaded him onto a gurney, and they took him away for further observation to the hospital. Now there's a little bit of humor that goes along with this story. I received a written commendation from the area manager to complement me for saving the life of a traveler.

Why is that humorous? It's humorous because the ambulance guys told me insulin was not what the kid needed. He was suffering from an insulin overdose, and I damn near killed him by giving him more.

He only needed orange juice or something sweet to break down the insulin. I was happy with the commendation, but there was no damn way in hell that I going to let my superiors know I had screwed up. It remained my secret even after I retired, but it's out now.

Part Eleven:
Life After Retirement

WE OWNED AN acreage, so to save on property tax we started a tree farm. One of the drawbacks of tree farming is that occasionally some asshole will try to steal a Christmas tree. To prevent that, I installed a seven-foot chain link fence around my entire property. I installed it with the sharp side of the chain link fence wire up so that anyone trying to climb over it would injure themselves while doing it.

Sure enough, I glanced out my window one day to see a guy scoot over the fence. By the time I got my shoes on and went out there, he had chopped three-quarters of the way through a beautiful blue spruce tree. He was still busy chopping as I approached him and surprised the hell out of him when I yelled, "What the fuck do you think you're doing!"

He looked up at me, jumped up, and threw his axe over the fence. Then he followed it, leaving part of his jacket torn off and hopefully a bit of stomach flesh on the sharp points of the chain links. He jumped into a waiting two-door Nissan sedan. The tree was about eight feet high with a bottom diameter of over six feet.

Use your imagination here. If I hadn't stopped this drunk, can you see him fighting to get that big tree over the fence because my seven-foot gate was also locked? Then how long do you think it would take a drunk to tie it to a Nissan with no roof rack? I should have stood back and watched the show because I lost the damn tree anyway.

Once we retired, we added three rooms onto our house to increase the square footage and re-configured the roof line to turn our bungalow into an executive home. We pulled it off too. Everything inside was brand new, Everything. We now had two bathrooms in our master bedroom. New roof, siding, windows etc. Chain link fence with electric gate around the entire 3.5 acres. Then we put it up for sale and because it was in a tourist area it sold for big bucks. We moved back to the coast where most of our kids lived. I bought a brand new Harley Davidson trike and I joined 4 different motorcycle clubs to see which group best suited me.

I'm getting fatter and lazier and my wife has turned into an exercise freak. She tries to encourage me to join in but I'm not a masochist and I have a TV and a motorcycle..

While riding with one of the groups, I lost my concentration and went over the edge of the road, planting the front wheel of the bike in the dirt sending me flying over the top of my bike. Then it flipped over and 900 pounds of motorcycle came crashing down on top of me jamming my left elbow under the hot muffler. It happened fast but to me it took forever. Everything seemed to go in slow motion. No matter what I did, I couldn't free my arm so the muffler kept burning into my elbow. The burn went deep and left a hole almost an inch in depth where a bolt on the muffler burned deep into the flesh.

Luckily I was riding with a group, and they saw me crash. Once they got the bike off me, I realized my elbow was dislocated. I picked up my left forearm with my right hand and I could swing it in every direction – even against the angle of the elbow joint – yet I felt no pain at all. I asked my riding buddies to take a picture. It was a bit embarrassing because the fire department and an ambulance showed up and six firefighters had to carry my 250-pound fat ass up the side of that bank on a canvas stretcher.

I was still holding onto my arm to keep it straight up and down at that time because it was starting to hurt. Once I got into the ambulance, the attendant that was assessing me was now holding my forearm perpendicular to my body. At that point I was shaking like I was an alcoholic suffering from lack of alcohol, and it looked like I had the DTs. I asked the ambulance guy, "Why in the hell am I shaking like this?" He told me it was because the adrenaline that my body had created was dissipating. I have no idea how that happens but now I was really feeling the pain.

The attendant told me he was going to place my arm across my chest for transport to the hospital. I told him, "There's no damn way I can let you do that because the pain is now intolerable." The poor guy held my arm up until we got to the hospital then I held it up myself until

I was sedated. When I awoke, my arm was bandaged and in a sling. I had to wear a cast for a few months and my elbow is now a bit deformed, but I consider myself very fortunate. I now have a scar that resembles an asshole where the bolt burned in. My wife says, "That scar suits you well." She must be kidding, right?

Last Part:
That's All Folks

THANK YOU FOR reading my book. Sorry about the crude language, but that was a genuine part of my life. I am aware that many of the actions and choices in my life constitute criminal behavior, but at the end of the day, I have to say I've done more good in my life than this book demonstrates. However, "good" isn't as interesting!

This book speaks mostly of things in my life that make me look like an ass. I'm not always an ass, but I have my moments. Truth be told, I would never walk past someone who is being attacked or who is injured, and I would never neglect to help a friend in need. My plans for the future are to spend quality time with my family, meet with my pals twice a week, and go on motorcycle trips with my wife and friends. When I get too old to get on my Harley, I'll be on the hunt for a hot rod, so I can go to car shows and bullshit with car people.

I wrote this book mainly for my future generations because I often wonder what kind of lives my grandfather lived or his father or even my own father before I was born.

I have more than enough material to write another book, but it wasn't easy writing this one. However, if this one gets attention, I will.

CPSIA information can be obtained
at www.ICGtesting.com
Printed in the USA
BVHW041008010920
587628BV00004B/16